Smokies ROAD GUIDE

by Jerry DeLaughter

GREAT SMOKY MOUNTAINS ASSOCIATION
GATLINBURG, TN

Edited by Rebecca Burks, Stan Canter, Kent Cave,
Don DeFoe, Steve Kemp, and Ed Purcell
Designed by Shelly Powell
Printed in China

5 6 7 8 9

ISBN 0-937207-00-4

GREAT SMOKY MOUNTAINS
ASSOCIATION

Great Smoky Mountains Association is a private,
nonprofit organization which supports the
educational, scientific, and historical programs of
Great Smoky Mountains National Park. Our
publications are an educational service intended to
enhance the public's understanding and enjoyment
of the national park. If you would like to know more
about our publications, memberships, guided hikes,
and other projects, please contact:

Great Smoky Mountains Association
115 Park Headquarters Road
Gatlinburg, Tennessee 37738
888 898-9102 or www.SmokiesInformation.org

Acknowledgments

A book such as this is a team effort, and necessarily eclectic. The writer's part is a pleasure: to read and absorb good information, to ride the roads and enjoy their beauties, and then to become a traveling companion-in-print, to share the sights and their stories with you.

The real work is done by others. They deserve my deepest appreciation, and yours. The people named here have spent great time and effort trying to help you enjoy and benefit from your Smokies experience, and to preserve that experience for your grandchildren. Our thanks to them.

First to the Great Smoky Mountains Association; and foremost to Rebecca Burks, the Association's talented publications director, patient editor, and friend. And to a dedicated park staff, especially Chief of Visitor Services Stan Canter and naturalist Don DeFoe; to Superintendent John Cook for loyal and valuable support, to Assistant Superintendent Ro Wauer, to Librarians Claryse Myers and Annette Hartigan, to Resource Management Chief Stu Coleman, and to many others on the park staff, known and unknown, who have helped to make this book a reality.

Another round of thanks belongs to those dedicated writers and researchers who have helped preserve the park's story. Much of the natural and human history shared in this book reflects their patient work, borrowed freely to share in this context. Some of these valuable works are unpublished monographs—Cataloochee, Cades Cove, and Warriors Path are notable among them. Others, including those listed at the end of this book, are available at any of the park's visitor centers.

And that brings us to a word of advice.

Stopping at the visitor centers is an indispensable part of any park visit. Excellent exhibits, a short motion picture, helpful staff, and plenty of books and pamphlets will multiply your pleasure many times over.

—Jerry DeLaughter

Contents

Introduction

Things worth seeing are worth knowing. The beauty of Great Smoky Mountains National Park is that it is a magnificent story as well as a magnificent place. The story, like the place, changes and continues. By your presence here, you are part of the story. These half-million acres are now yours, preserved as a precious resource for the enrichment of all people who come to see and to know. That enrichment requires no greater effort on your part than a receptive spirit.

It's the aim of this book to enhance your personal discovery, whether this is your first trip or your fiftieth. As return visitors know well, each trip is new, with new joy. Different seasons, different weather conditions, even different times of day provide wholly new perspectives on the park's beauty.

Many wonders await discovery, including a number from the comfort of your vehicle. Most visitors follow Newfound Gap Road through the park and its spur leading to Clingmans Dome. Many also enjoy the scenic Little River drive. These are worthwhile and shouldn't be missed.

Yet, sojourns into the wilderness are not for backcountry hikers alone. Did you know that many special places can be reached by vehicle as well? A nature trail just for cars, for instance.

Uncrowded roads that take you to secluded coves of great beauty, or high along mountain ridges where the park seems yours alone. A scenic foothills drive offering vistas of the park impossible anywhere else. Roads into the heart of the backcountry, excursions into the wilderness you might have thought impossible in the confines of a car.

Each is special and offers an intimate acquaintance with the park. They are the "less-traveled roads" that, as the poet Robert Frost said, "can make all the difference."

DRIVING DISTANCES TO THE NATIONAL PARK

Approximate mileages to the national park boundary from:

Atlanta, GA—175

Birmingham, AL—300

Charleston, WV—315

Charlotte, NC—165

Chattanooga, TN—125

Chicago, IL—580

Cincinnati, OH—325

Durham, NC—285

Greenville, SC—110

Huntsville, AL—250

Indianapolis, IN—395

Jackson, MS—550

Jacksonville, FL—450

Louisville, KY—290

Memphis, TN—425

Nashville, TN—230

Tampa-St. Pete, FL—640

Auto Touring in the Smoky Mountains

Great Smoky Mountains National Park is America's most visited national park and encompasses over 800 square miles. Times when visitation is highest are June 15-August 15 and October (especially October weekends). During these times, traffic may become congested, especially on the Newfound Gap and Cades Cove Loop roads.

Auto tours of the park offer a variety of experiences, including panoramic views, tumbling mountain streams, weathered historic buildings, and mature hardwood forests stretching to the horizon.

There are over 270 miles of road—detailed in this book—to choose from in the Smokies. Most are paved, and even the gravel roads are maintained in suitable condition for standard passenger cars. Travel speeds on most of the park's paved roads average 30 miles per hour.

■ DRIVING TIPS

Driving in the mountains presents new challenges for many drivers. When traveling uphill on hot days, watch your engine temperature carefully to make sure it is not overheating. If overheating occurs, rest your vehicle at a pullout before continuing.

When going downhill, shift to a lower gear to conserve your brakes and avoid brake failure. If your vehicle has an automatic transmission, use "L" or "2." Keep an extra cushion of distance between you and the vehicle in front of you as protection against sudden stops. In summer, motorists can also avoid the crowds by traveling before 10 a.m. or after 5 p.m. During October, traffic is heaviest during the afternoons and evenings.

Watch for animals crossing roads, especially at night. Scores of bears and other animals are killed by motorists every year. Following posted speed limits will reduce your chances of hitting wildlife.

As a courtesy to other park visitors, slow moving vehicles should use pullouts to let other cars pass. Pullouts are located every mile or so on most park roads.

There are no gas stations or other related services available in the park. Complete services are available in Cherokee, NC, Gatlinburg, TN, and Townsend, TN. In the event of an emergency, call 911. For non-emergency calls to park headquarters, dial (865) 436-1200.

SAFE WINTER DRIVING

When driving downhill on a snowy or icy road, shift to a lower gear ("2", "1", or "low" for automatic transmissions) to avoid using your brakes more than is necessary. When you do brake, apply pressure gently and smoothly.

Drive defensively. Leave extra room between your vehicle and the vehicle in front of you. Be prepared for sudden stops and erratic action by other drivers. Allow extra distance for braking.

If you become stuck, don't gun the engine or spin your tires—you'll only become more deeply mired. Rock the car by shifting between forward and reverse gears and applying gentle pressure to the gas pedal.

■ ROAD CLOSURES

Cades Cove Loop Road, Parson Branch Road, Roaring Fork Motor Nature Trail, Rich Mountain Road and part of the Cataloochee Valley road are closed from sunset to sunrise. All other roads are open day and night.

Several of the park's roads are closed in winter. Others may close temporarily due to weather. Below are the approximate open times for seasonal roads.

Balsam Mountain Road
mid-May through late October

Clingmans Dome Road
April 1 through November 30

Parson Branch Road
mid-March through mid-November

Rich Mountain Road
mid-May through mid-November

Roaring Fork Nature Trail
mid-March through November 30

Although the National Park Service attempts to keep Newfound Gap Road open year-round, temporary, weather-related closures do occur. If the road is closed, stop at a nearby visitor center for information on alternative routes between North Carolina and Tennessee. Passage may be limited to vehicles with tire chains or four-wheel drive when snowy conditions exist. Little River and Cades Cove Loop roads are rarely closed by inclement weather.

■ Quiet Walkways

Selected trails scattered throughout the park are designated as Quiet Walkways. These paths are designed to encourage motorists to stop and enjoy a short stroll in a mountain forest. Most parking areas for Quiet Walkways are only large enough for two or three vehicles, assuring users a sense of relative solitude.

■ Theft

Theft from parked cars is a perennial problem in most national parks. Thieves almost always target purses, cameras, laptop computers, portable stereos, and other easily exchangeable commodities. The best defense is to keep valuables on your person. Locking them out of sight in your trunk may be effective, but then again most trunks are also easily broken into. Be aware that thieves may be in the parking area watching as you slip your purse into the glove box or stow your video camera in the trunk. Do not leave a note on your dashboard saying how long you will be hiking. Notify park rangers by calling (865) 436-1294 or 436-1230 to report a theft or suspicious activity.

■ Park Regulations

Picking, digging, or damaging plants is prohibited. Feeding wildlife and improper food storage are illegal.

Pets are not permitted on most park trails. They are allowed in campgrounds, picnic areas, parking areas, and along roads if leashed.

Writing or carving on historic buildings or natural features (including trees) is punishable by fine and imprisonment.

■ KEY

Each chapter features a key with symbols that indicate things that you can expect to find on a particular route. Those symbols are defined below:

▲	Campground	⛫	Observation Tower
🚶	Hiking Trail	🌲	Picnic Area
🏚	Historic Structures	👫	Ranger Station
🐎	Horse Stables	🚻	Restrooms
🚶	Interpretive Trail	?	Visitor Information

How to Use This Road Guide

As you drive through the park you'll notice small posts at pullouts, most bearing a color and a number. They correspond to the points of interest discussed in this road guide. The color identifies the road, and the suggested stops are numbered in sequence along your route.

An exception is Newfound Gap Road. It is delineated by mile posts, one each mile starting at the park boundary in Gatlinburg, TN and ending at the boundary with Cherokee, NC. If you're entering the park via the parkway in Gatlinburg and you want to set your tripometer, hit zero at the point where the backyard of the Applewood Restaurant meets the national park. The points of interest in this book are keyed to miles traveled south from Gatlinburg. There are not numbered posts for each point of interest, but the mile posts will help you locate them.

Several park roads may be traveled in either direction, depending on your starting point. If you should be headed in the direction opposite the sequence of numbers, simply follow the numbered stops in reverse order. Most routes are introduced by a solid color marker.

Refer to the map enclosed in the back cover of this book to get your bearings, and look through the text to select tours of interest. As you use the guide, keep these important points in mind:

—Each road is different, and offers its own experience. Don't miss those less-traveled roads. Get away from the crowds and make new discoveries.

—Browse through the whole guide, whether or not you plan to take all its routes. You may be enticed to explore new areas. And you'll certainly learn a lot more by reading about the park's great variety of attractions. In addition, tidbits of useful information are sprinkled through the text to enhance your visit.

First Auto Invades Great Smokies 1914-15

This article was published in the Maryville-Alcoa Times September 12, 1963.

The name Fisher is as important in early automobile firsts in Blount County as it is to the nation's automobile body industry. Blount's Fisher is A. J., retired superintendent of Schlosser Tannery at Walland who lives at 314 E. High St., Maryville, TN.

A lover of the Smokies and the sixth Blount Countian to own an automobile, Fisher was the first to take a car to Cades Cove, first to take one up Bote Mountain and probably the person who inspired the first party to take one to Spence Field.

Fisher, who still enjoys visiting remote areas in the Smokies, took the picture below of his 1912 Cadillac on the Anderson Trail, headed toward Spencer's Cabin October 12, 1914 during the ascent of Bote Mountain. Bote Mountain is one of the main ridges running down off Thunderhead Mountain, the peak astride the Tennessee-North Carolina line which dominates the Smoky skyline as viewed from the Maryville-Alcoa area.

At the wheel of the car is the late W. W. Blazer with D. Otis Waters at right in the front seat. Left to right in the backseat is J. S. Dunn and George P. Walker.

The men took the car up the mountain even though there wasn't much resembling a road to the top. They had to use a block and tackle and chains on the rear tires to get the car over the 8- to 10-foot high fall on Farr Branch.

The same car, which Fisher purchased in June 1913, was the first in Cades Cove, the trip being made September 26, 1915. Otis Waters, Guy Smithson, and Levi Walker left Walland with Fisher for Cades Cove at 9:15 a.m. There were no bridges for automobiles between Walland and

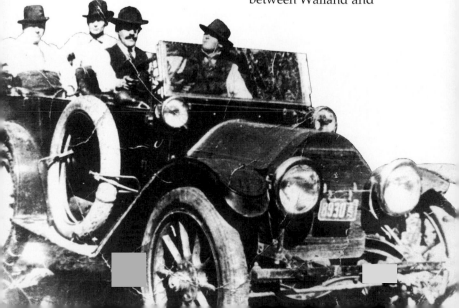

Townsend. Little River had to be crossed several times so Fisher chose September when the river would be at its lowest level and the dirt road across Rich Mountain would be in its best condition.

The 37 x 5 tires helped keep the car high enough

returned to Walland that same day without having to light the acetylene-burning headlights.

The picture [below] shows the first motor vehicle in Spence Field was a Chevrolet pickup truck belonging to the government. It was taken there in 1933 by a group headed by

First and only motor vehicle in Spence Field up to 1952.

above the ground to clear boulders sticking up in the road and to get across streams without drowning out the motor. Despite the undependability of tires in those days and the habit cars had of heating up, the group had no trouble on either score that day.

A letter from The Times correspondent at Walland and published on page one October 7, 1915 told of the incident. The report stated that when the Fisher party reached Cades Cove, Mr. and Mrs. Witt Shields, Kale Wilcox, Mrs. George Shields and children were taken for a ride into the upper end of the cove. It was the first automobile ride for all but Uncle Witt Shields.

No other car had crossed those mountains. The party

Chief Park Ranger Charles Dunn, who is now retired and lives in Dry Valley. Included in the group were several WPA workers.

Fisher, who at the time was head of Camp 11 of the Civilian Conservation Corps (CCC) in Cades Cove, had planned to drive a car to Spence Field the following day. Recalling the incident, Fisher chuckled and added that Dunn heard of his plans and beat him to the draw. Although Fisher didn't attempt the trip after Dunn had scored the first, Fisher has a copy of the picture of Dunn and the pickup truck at Spence Field and treasures it as much as if he had been the first one there.

Newfound Gap Road

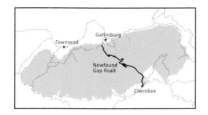

The drive across the mountains is the park's most-traveled road and its popularity is justified. Views are memorable as you follow the West Prong of the Little Pigeon River up from the 1,462-foot elevation at Sugarlands to 5,046 feet above sea level at Newfound Gap, then descend 3,000 feet to Oconaluftee, 16 miles away. It's an easy ascent, although the road requires two tunnels and an unusual 360-degree loop over itself to make the climb.

Unlike other roads described in this book, Newfound Gap Road (U.S. 441) is delineated by mile posts. They are placed one each mile starting at the park boundary in Gatlinburg, TN and ending at the boundary with Cherokee, NC. If you're entering the park via the parkway in Gatlinburg and you want to set your tripometer, hit zero at the point where the backyard of the Applewood Restaurant meets the national park, mile post 0. The points of interest in this chapter are keyed to miles traveled south from Gatlinburg. There are not numbered posts for each point of interest, but the mile posts will help you locate them.

Left:
The northern entrance to Great Smoky Mountains National Park, near Gatlinburg, TN.

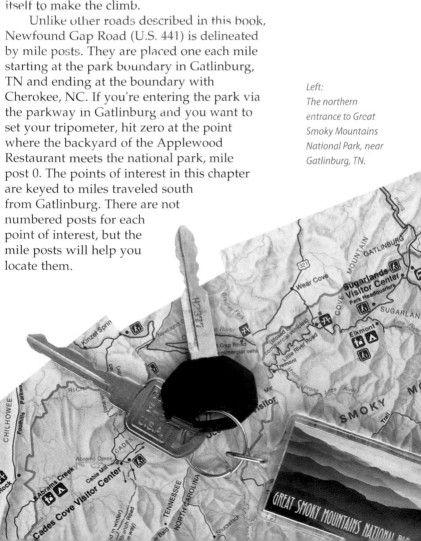

● MILE POST 1.7
SUGARLANDS VISITOR CENTER

This rich valley along the Little Pigeon River's West Prong was among the earliest Euro-American settlements on the Tennessee side of the Smokies. By the early 1800s a number of families had established homes here and a few miles downstream at White Oak Flats, now Gatlinburg. This area was called "Sugar Lands" because of its abundance of sugar maple trees.

Today Sugarlands Visitor Center welcomes hundreds of thousands of visitors annually, and a stop here is indispensable to a meaningful Smokies experience. Folders, guidebooks, camping and hiking permits, and other materials are provided, and a short film will help you get acquainted with the area. A special feature is an extraordinary nature exhibit providing an introduction to the abundance of life in the park.

Sugarlands is one of three visitor centers in the park. Others are at Oconaluftee, near Cherokee at the North Carolina entrance, and at Cable Mill in Cades Cove.

The Fighting Creek Self-guiding Nature Trail at Sugarlands offers a glimpse into life in these flats before the park was created: rocky fields, a log cabin, the efforts of people making lives for themselves in a wild country. Just past the visitor center on Newfound Gap Road is the Sugarlands Valley Nature Trail, a fully-accessible, paved walkway with really interesting tactile exhibits and a special large-print folder.

Left:
An assortment of field guides available at visitor centers in or near the park

Right, from top:
View from Campbell Overlook; Carlos Campbell; a family enjoys a barbeque at Chimneys Picnic Area

GATLINBURG TRAIL

Gatlinburg was named for Radford Gatlin, a local merchant who kept the town's post office in his store in the mid 1850s. He was an unpopular Confederate sympathizer who agreed to leave town under the condition that the town be named for him. The town was formerly called White Oak Flats. This popular 1.7-mile trail runs from Sugarlands Visitor Center to the Gatlinburg city limits.

● MILE POST 3.9
CAMPBELL OVERLOOK

This point is named in honor of Carlos Campbell, conservationist, author, and a moving force in the park's creation. The roadside exhibit is an excellent guide to the different forest patterns in the mountains before you. The near peak on the left is Bull Head and the distant peak in the center of your view is Balsam Point.

It's been said that driving up to Newfound Gap from the lowlands is the botanical equivalent of a trip from Georgia north to Canada. The display here clearly demonstrates those latitudinal changes represented on the vertical slopes of the Smokies, from mixed southern hardwoods to Canadian-zone evergreens.

● MILE POST 6.2
CHIMNEYS PICNIC AREA & COVE HARDWOOD NATURE TRAIL

Here the Little Pigeon River is a rushing cascade, its banks lined with giant hemlocks and other trees—remnants of an old-growth forest, saved by the park's creation. This is a dramatic setting, worth a pause for a picnic and a stroll along the self-guiding nature trail.

The area takes its name from the towering Chimney Tops, twin peaks rising abruptly beyond it. Here too is a good opportunity to get acquainted with one of the most diverse of nature's communities, the cove hardwood forest.

This self-guiding trail is a moderate three-quarter mile loop, beginning just after you enter the picnic grounds. The sheltered cove, actually a kind of ravine, is unusual because of the accumulation of rich humus in its crevice, which also gathers much runoff from rainfall and forms a natural course for springs and streams. In this deep, rich soil, protected from climatic extremes, life in the cove is marked by variety and abundance. A leaflet at the trailhead will guide you through this special place.

● MILE POST 7.1
CHIMNEY TOPS OVERLOOKS

These three overlooks provide outstanding views of one of the park's best-known features. A roadside exhibit at one of the overlooks describes the twin peaks known to the Cherokee as Duniskwal-guni (forked antlers). They cap a sheer rise of nearly 2,000 feet, one of the Smokies' steepest cliffs. The right-hand peak has a cavity in its top about 30 feet deep, the "flue" which inspires the present name.

Directly across from the overlooks, road cuts have exposed an impressive wall of clearly layered rock. This is a good chance to see how the earth beneath you has been laid down, lifted, and tilted over the past half-billion years or so.

Left, from top:
Hikers on Chimney
Tops Trail; Sharp-
lobed hepatica;
Newfound Gap
Road

Right:
Cove hardwood
forest

● **MILE POST 7.9**
COVE HARDWOOD ROADSIDE EXHIBIT

Here's a pretty spot to pause, enjoy the rushing river, and read the informative roadside exhibit. Stop and consider: the abundance of life in the park is obvious; less apparent (and overlooked by casual visitors) is the variety of its communities! These moist, sheltered coves are among the richest forest communities on this continent, home to many different species of trees and a wide variety of animals and small plants.

In the woods across the road, big angular rocks are exposed among the trees. During the Pleistocene ice age, the huge pieces were split by frost from rock ledges higher on the slopes. Overgrown by forest and lichen-covered today, these boulder deposits are relics of a colder time, a period when permanent snow fields dotted mountains like Le Conte.

For its variety and abundance, life in the Smokies depends on a thin layer of soil, which varies in depth from a few inches to several feet, all spread tenuously atop a solid rock core reaching nine miles deep in this mass of mountains. That's why seemingly small changes on the face of the land can make a drastic difference to the delicate balance.

● MILE POST 8.6
CHIMNEY TOPS TRAIL

This parking area is access to a popular, but strenuous, trail that climbs to the top of the Chimneys. It's a four-mile roundtrip leading through a magnificent virgin forest, then a steep 1,335-foot climb up to a rewarding panorama, and a peek into the "flue" of the Chimneys.

The trail begins along an ancient route. The first people to venture into the high country no doubt followed the stream up from the lowlands, just as Newfound Gap Road now does. Here at the parking area, the trail veered right to follow the creek you see feeding the Little Pigeon River at this point, and climbed sharply upward to cross the heart of the mountains at Indian Gap. The first wagon roads, more than 150 years ago, followed the well-used Indian trail. The present Newfound Gap route was built in the 1920s.

● MILE POST 10.1
STREAM EXHIBIT

Waterways like the Little Pigeon River, plus the dozens of others that course through the mountains, are important to life's abundance in the Smokies. This roadside exhibit demonstrates that graphically. So, as you enjoy the beauty of the mountain streams, give a thought to their vitality as well. They're the lifeblood of the park.

Before you complain about the weather (fog and rain are fairly common), remember that abundant moisture is critical to abundant

Vehicle break-ins sometimes occur at trailheads. Lock your car and keep purses, cameras, portable stereos, and other valuables on your person or lock them in the trunk before you get to the trailhead.

Left and right: Views from Chimney Tops Trail

THE LOOP

This is difficult engineering even now; think of the obstacles faced by road builders with hand tools! Here the mountains crowd the Little Pigeon River closely on both sides, leaving little room for a road. To provide passage, a tunnel had to be cut and the road had to make a super-switchback, actually looping back atop itself in a 360-degree circuit to "stairstep" its way up the steep slope.

A second interpretation of the loop came from local wag and mountain guide, Wiley Oakley. He claimed that when the road was built, there was some left over, so they "tied a knot in it."

life. And not only here. The 900 billion gallons that fall in the Smokies each year are also vitally important far beyond the park; feeding rivers, watering land, helping provide electricity, nourishing life throughout the Tennessee and Mississippi river valleys as the water courses its way first west, then north, and finally south toward the Gulf of Mexico. The park includes 28 watersheds with minimal disturbance, producing some of the cleanest water in the eastern United States.

As you step carefully among the rocks for a closer look, scoop up a handful of the precious liquid and let it trickle through your fingers. Notice how cold and clear, born as it is in deep springs high up the mountainside. The sparkling droplets seem so light and gentle, but during floods when they're laden with silt, they hold enormous power. The great gorge you're driving was carved patiently, millennium after millennium, by the force of this water. Even now it does its work. The giant rocks around you are carried downward by the water's force, their rocky edges ground smooth by its timeless sculpture.

The little tumbling stream has been steadfastly at work for many eons before you

Left, from top:
Alum Cave Bluffs; a
small foot bridge
crosses Styx Branch

Right:
Mt. Le Conte

came; it will continue for eons more after you leave this spot. For the moment you're here, absorb its wonder.

● MILE POST 10.4
ALUM CAVE TRAIL

There's a good reason this is such a popular stopping place. Several good reasons, actually, since it's the portal to rewarding walks, hikes, and climbs to suit almost any timetable and ability.

The shorter version (2.5 miles round-trip) is a fairly level walk along picturesque Alum Cave Creek through a peaceful hardwood forest that leads to Arch Rock, a natural tunnel created by weathering.

To continue to Alum Cave Bluffs, stay on the trail right through Arch Rock for another three-quarters of a mile. It's a bit more rugged than the shorter version, but well worth the time.

The "cave" is actually a large overhanging bluff, and site of a commercial venture in the heart of the Smokies 150 years ago.

Here the Epsom Salts Company mined Epsom salts and "pseudo-alum" but found the project too expensive and soon abandoned it. During the Civil War several hundred men supposedly extracted saltpeter from the bluffs for use in Confederate gunpowder.

Today it's a trail full of discoveries of another kind, not the least of which are the occasional ravens who seem to delight in diving down the face of Alum Cave Bluffs to catch the updraft and ride the wind back up again.

Past Alum Cave Bluffs the trail leads onward and upward to Mt. Le Conte, a three-mile hike that's strenuous, but still the shortest (and to many hikers the most scenic) route up the mountain. That's a daylong outing at least—overnight at the lodge (with advance reservations) is better still—but the views are some of the park's finest and the trip is unforgettable.

Le Conte is unique as the site of the most popular inn in the east not accessible by car. The summit can be reached only on foot. But the lodge on top is a perennial attraction, and reservations are a must (call 865-429-5704). Many who make the trip are drawn back again and again.

Whether you want a short stroll in the woods or a climb to Mt. Le Conte, do linger for a walk across the wooden bridge.

Even from the road, the variety of vegetation is apparent. The elevation at the parking area (3,850 feet) was the edge of the timberline during the peak of the Ice Ages. Above 4,000 feet between here and the crest at Newfound Gap the land was treeless. Even now the higher vegetation is more stunted than that below, and high-altitude evergreens join the community.

MT. LE CONTE, ELEVATION 6,593'

MT. LE CONTE

Named for John Le Conte, a Georgia-born physician and professor of chemistry, physics, and natural history. The mountain was named by Samuel Buckley in appreciation for John Le Conte's assistance in determining its elevation in the 1850s. John was one of the persons who helped take barometer readings at lower elevations at exactly the same time that Buckley was taking readings on top of the mountain. The difference of these readings was used to calculate the elevation of the peak.

Now that the earth's climate is warmer, vegetation cloaks the highest peaks. At this latitude in today's climate, the Smokies would have to be twice their present height to reach the treeless timberline.

Left, from top: Newfound Gap Road; Anakeesta Ridge landslide

Right: Sunset from Morton Overlook

● MILE POST 13.2 (NORTHBOUND)/ 13.5 (SOUTHBOUND) VIEW OF LANDSLIDE

The mountain scene seems so permanent, but change is constantly going on. Most changes are so slow they're imperceptible in a human lifetime. Occasionally, as is dramatically evident here, they are momentous.

Huge landslides across the valley bared the face of Anakeesta ("place of the balsams") Ridge in 1975 and 1993. The bare rock scar is mute testimony not only to constant change, but also to the delicate balance in which life itself is held.

● MILE POST 14.0 MORTON OVERLOOK

It would be hard to find more photogenic or inspiring views in the park than these. This overlook is named in honor of Ben A. Morton, Knoxville's mayor in the 1920s and an avid supporter of the effort to create a park here.

The distinctive Chimney Tops are easy to spot on your left. They, like Mt. Mingus (the highest peak on your left), are part of a long ridge called Sugarland Mountain, which runs down from the crest of the Smokies toward Gatlinburg, hidden by peaks in the lowlands 15 miles away.

Between the lofty peaks, the Little Pigeon River cuts its patient way through the rocks. Clinging to its banks, and sometimes to the cliffs themselves, is the road you travel.

● MILE POST 14.4
NORTHERN HARDWOODS FOREST

Where mountainsides meet to form a crevice, like this one followed by Walker Prong, it's called a "run" in mountain parlance. About a half-mile up this run, nearly 6,000 feet above sea level, abundant cold springs give rise to these picturesque headwaters of the Little Pigeon River.

The forest community nurtured by these waters is distinct from those below you. A casual visitor looking at the verdure of the mountains will see only a solid green carpet of abundant forest. True enough, but pause to look a little more closely.

How many different shades of green can you detect? How many different textures can you find in the great variety of foliage-little leaves, big leaves, thick or thin, gossamer or substantive? The "solid" carpet is actually a rich mosaic.

At this elevation northern hardwoods dominate—the type of forest you'd find, for instance, in upper New York and much of New England. Evergreen fir and spruce, which rule the higher slopes here, mix with broad-leaved hardwoods, chiefly American beech and yellow birch. This is near the upper limit of such trees as maples, black cherry, and hemlock; pin cherries, buckeyes, and serviceberry persist a little higher. And this altitude marks the beginning of the reign of Fraser fir and red spruce, mixed with the shrubby mountain ash.

In spring the understory is alive with spring-beauty, bluets, trilliums, and a variegated abundance of ferns and shrubs. River bottom, protected cove, mountain slope or summit; each of the Smokies' many worlds is a pleasure to discover. Linger a while to share them.

● MILE POST 14.7
NEWFOUND GAP

Out west this would be a "pass," but in New England a "notch." Such terms refer to low points that provide passage across the crests of mountains.

For many generations, until surveys proved otherwise, the Indian Gap two miles west of here was thought to be the lowest in the heart of the mountains. When this point (at 5,046 feet elevation) was discovered to be the lower, it was referred to as the "new-found gap."

Left, from top:
Pin cherry; a striking view from Thomas Divide on Newfound Gap Road; Laura Spelman Rockefeller Memorial at Newfound Gap

Right:
President Franklin Roosevelt giving the park dedication speech at Newfound Gap, September 2, 1940

This mainline Smokies ridge is the state line and also the route of the famous Appalachian Trail. Of the trail's 2,174 miles from Maine to Georgia, 71 follow a path through the park's high country.

The gap not only provides outstanding views in many directions, but also is a spot full of meaning. Here you might stand on the rock platform, as President Franklin Roosevelt did in 1940, to reflect on what has been granted to us and what our bequest to the future should be.

NEWFOUND GAP,
ELEVATION 5,046'

Consider with gratitude the Cherokee whose land this was; the Euro-Americans who settled it, and whose descendants gave up their homes for the nation to enjoy; botanist William Bartram, who dreamed of such a preserve 200 years ago; geographer Arnold Henry Guyot, who mapped the wild country; and the countless individuals, famous or unknown, who devoted much of their lives and energies to reclaiming the land and preserving it for the future.

Give special thought to Goldie Cox, Walter Grigsby, and John D. Rockefeller Jr. You may not recognize the first two names, but their legacy is here too. They are among the thousands of school children who in the 1920s donated "Pennies for the Park" to help inspire its creation.

Among those who responded was Rockefeller, the philanthropist whose $5 million gift finally made it possible to buy the thousands of separate parcels of land, and thus preserve these 800 square miles of matchless wilderness that you enjoy today.

APPALACHIAN TRAIL

The Appalachian Trail meanders through the mountains from Maine to Georgia, including 71 miles through the highlands of the Great Smokies. According to park archives, this trail was the first development in the park for the benefit of the public. Newfound Gap marks a popular intersection of the renowned trail.

The gap, 16 miles from Gatlinburg, 18 miles from Cherokee, is a good place to linger (but be extra careful around the parking area and on reentering the road). Learn more about the park from several exhibits along the overlook.

● MILE POST 15.4 OCONALUFTEE VALLEY OVERLOOK

At this point you're perched atop Thomas Divide, a high ridge running in an arc from Deep Creek (near Bryson City) to the crest of the Smokies just above. Newfound Gap Road, which follows the Oconaluftee River for most of its course up from Cherokee, climbs to the divide in a giant switchback just below, an S-curve that reverses your direction twice.

When the highway was built, its route followed the stream straight up the mountain below Thomas Divide. In the early 1960s that steeper version with its sharp hairpin curve was replaced by the wider loop and a more scenic drive along the top of the ridge.

Looking down the long ridge at the highway ribbon far below and into the undulating countryside in the misty distance,

Left, from top:
Sugar maple;
Newfound Gap Road through northern hardwood forest; view from Newfound Gap Road; Columbine

Right:
Traffic along Newfound Gap Road at Oconaluftee Valley Overlook

you may appreciate the reaction of a former visitor here.

It's said that a mountain man made his first-ever trip over the Smokies when the road was new, after spending his whole life in the Tennessee hollows. At this point in the drive he gazed long into the vast country below him and said, "If the world's as big back thataways as it is out yonder, then she's a whopper!"

● MILE POST 17.1 WILDERNESS EXHIBIT

Why do people, when they climb a mountain, call it "conquering" the peak? Or if they build a road or a farm, they have "tamed" the wilderness? Such terms may serve the human ego, but they also fortify the fallacy that people are at war with the world they live in. As this roadside exhibit illustrates, you can learn much on your visit here, if you pause to reflect.

Many among the country's great natural preserves were set aside while still in their natural states. Here in the Smokies, a natural treasure that had already been populated and commercially exploited was bought back by the public and allowed to return to a wild state.

THOMAS DIVIDE

Named for Colonel William Holland Thomas, friend and ally to the Cherokee. He was a land speculator who commanded the Cherokee troops who joined the Confederate Army during the Civil War. Because Cherokee could not, by law, purchase or own land at the time, he purchased 50,000 acres for them. This became the nucleus of the Qualla Boundary or Reservation, home of the Eastern Band of the Cherokee. Thomas was adopted by the Cherokee tribe and with the death of their chief in 1839, he became chief. Thomas was an attorney, entrepreneur and railroad promoter, and he served from 1848 to 1861 as a North Carolina State Senator.

Some traces of humanity are preserved for their historic value. Such preservation requires diligence, however, since the land is always ready to heal itself and erase all evidence of such temporary "taming" by humans.

The most lasting souvenirs you can take home are these bits of wisdom. That the best way to live with the world is in harmony, not conflict. That for all its wild strength, the natural world is in delicate balance, and scars are easy to leave and slow to heal. That all forms of life must share the planet, but only one form has the reasoning intelligence, and thus the responsibility, to use it wisely for the future's sake.

**WEBB OVERLOOK,
ELEVATION 4,500'**

● MILE POST 17.7
WEBB OVERLOOK

This overlook honors the memory of Asheville newspaper publisher Charles A. Webb, civic leader and conservationist whose efforts helped establish Great Smoky Mountains National Park. From this point due south, you're looking down the valley of Deep Creek toward Bryson City (nine miles distant).

You also have a good view—weather permitting— of the park's highest peak, Clingmans Dome, which should be easy to spot a little south of due west. The distinctive "backbone" of the mainline Smokies covers 70 miles from its abrupt rise from the valley of the Little Tennessee on the west to the Pigeon River gorge on the east. Its average elevation is nearly a mile above sea level, and 16 park peaks exceed 6,000 feet.

Marvelous country for soaring birds, you might think—and you'd be right. Those you may see include the Turkey Vulture, whose six-foot wingspan is nearly that of an eagle, and any of a variety of hawks.

Or the ravens. Similar to a crow but larger, the Common Raven symbolizes the high wilderness perhaps better than any other bird. They're rarely seen in the eastern United States, except here in the southern Appalachian mountaintops. Ravens may dive sharply into an updraft only to ride the wind up again, perhaps uttering their loud *krrruk!* or a musical *tonk!*, apparently in the sheer joy of freedom in the wild.

Eagles and falcons were a common part of this high-flying community, but as humans destroyed the surrounding wilderness and killed those majestic raptors for "sport," their numbers were decimated. Thanks to a concerted effort by the National Park Service, the Peregrine Fund, and many others, Peregrine Falcons are again nesting and rearing young atop jagged Smoky Mountain cliffs. Golden Eagles, Bald Eagles, and Osprey are also being returned to other areas of the southern Appalachians.

Such belated wisdom—a kind of atonement—may have awakened in our species just in time for the sake of your grandchildren. Places like the Smokies make it possible to hope.

Left:
Newfound Gap Road at Deep Creek Overlook

Right, from top:
Catawba Rhododendron; sunset from Webb Overlook

● Mile Post 18.5
Logging Exhibit

In one sense, logging devastated the great Smokies, but the destruction of these vast old-growth forests led at last to enough public alarm to demand preservation. This exhibit tells something of the logging story; the most important human factor affecting these mountains.

First effects were relatively small: clearing for farms and pastures, from early pioneers until about a hundred years ago. Commercial cutting began with selective removal of rare cabinet woods: walnut, cherry, birch, and hickory. With the nation's growth at the turn of the 20th century came enormous demand for construction timber—oak, tuliptree, and pine. And finally pulpwood (which included almost everything else) for paper and other uses.

Wholesale timber operations meant a vast network of railroads, lumber camps, and villages. And vulnerable bare land, exploited streams, logging roads, dangerous brush fires. It's hard to realize now, looking at this dense

blanket of growth, that more than three-fourths of these lush contours (about 400,000 acres) were logged away, mostly in a scant 20-year period after 1900.

When, in the late 1920s, the drive began to preserve the land, nearly half of the acreage in what is now the park was owned by two lumber companies and most of the rest by seven others.

Here and there throughout the park are precious cathedral stands of majestic trees, vestiges of a grandeur that once cloaked the mountains. Given time and human care, the land heals itself; after 70 years, the evidence is before you.

● MILE POST 23.4
OCONALUFTEE RIVER

It's pronounced "oh-kon-a-LUF-tee," and the name seems almost as long as the river itself. To the Cherokee, Ekwanulti means place-by-the-river. Corrupted through generations of unfamiliar tongues, it became "Oconaluftee." In local parlance the name is often abbreviated as "Lufty."

Road builders, like rivers, seek the easiest course through the mountains. Newfound Gap Road follows the Oconaluftee River almost all the way to its headwaters near Newfound Gap. Less than a mile from the Lufty's source, other springs give rise to its sister stream across the mountain, the West Prong of the Little Pigeon River. The Lufty flows south, the Pigeon north, but both turn west.

Left, from top:
Little River Railroad;
loggers falling a tree
with a crosscut saw;
sawmill at
Smokemont;
logging aftermath

Right, from top:
Locomotive No. 105;
snaking out a log
with a team of oxen;
Locomotive No. 148

The two rivers flow in opposite directions, since they begin on opposite sides of the mainline Smokies ridge. And that illustrates an oddity about streams in these

mountains: no matter which direction they flow, they all wind up heading west.

That's because the Smokies are not a "divide" in the continental sense. That role is played by the Blue Ridge Mountains south and east of here, where the waters' flow is divided between the Atlantic Ocean and the Gulf of Mexico.

The streams here are all part of the Tennessee River drainage area, and have meandered through the mountains over eons. The nature of the land dictates their course, but also requires that all feed the Tennessee River.

Enjoy these quiet moments getting acquainted with the mountain streams. Step carefully among the rocks, look closely at protected eddies, and marvel at the resourceful little water bugs that manage to make their living there. Watch slender leaves ride the rapids. Think about the water rushing by, shaping and nourishing the land and its life on its long trip to flow eventually— more than 2,000 miles and maybe a month from now—into the Gulf of Mexico at New Orleans.

Or just sit and listen, as the rush of water shuts out the sound of the other world and draws you into its peace.

● Mile Post 25.4
Collins Creek Picnic Area

Here's a lovely spot for lunch, or just to pause and enjoy a Quiet Walkway in the woods. The little creek that gives the place its name has special meaning in the Smokies.

Robert Collins lived around here 150 years ago. A rugged mountain man, he was gatekeeper on the old 'Lufty Turnpike, which climbed the mountains from the Cherokee lowlands. Collins knew these uncharted hills like the lines in his weathered hands and served as guide for Dr. Arnold Henry Guyot, the noted Swiss cartographer who mapped the wilderness.

With Guyot on horseback behind him, Bobby Collins hacked his way up to the highest of the peaks and across the ridges, leading the scientist to places he knew so well.

They were an odd couple, poles apart in language and culture, background, and education. However, they worked and ate and slept together in the wild high country for weeks on end, united by a common affection for this timeless place.

Guyot gave names to many of the park's peaks and other features. In fitting tribute to his loyal companion, Guyot named a towering mountain and a humble creek in Collins' honor.

Left, from top: Winged elm; winter mountain stream

Right, from top: Visitors enjoy lunch at Collins Creek Picnic Area; dogwood tree blossom; sawmill at Smokemont, circa 1930, prior to becoming a park campground

● MILE POST 27.2
SMOKEMONT CAMPGROUND & NATURE TRAIL

This broad, flat area was first an early settlement called "Bradleytown." Later it became a busy logging village, sawmill, and railroad terminus for spurs that climbed the coves to haul down the forest. Now, as one of the park's most popular campgrounds, it's a village of another sort.

The stream through Smokemont is Bradley Fork, named for an early Euro-American settler. "Fork" and "prong" are mountain terms referring to tributaries that feed a larger stream. "Creek" and "branch" are also used for small watercourses; around the South you don't usually hear them called "stream" or "brook."

All the land from here across Newfound Gap to the Chimney Tops, and from Clingmans Dome to Mt. Guyot to the east, was part of Champion Fibre's vast holdings prior to 1931. The lumber company's land, nearly 93,000 acres in the heart of the Smokies, was the largest single tract among those bought for the park. All traces of the old logging village have given way to the campground. But it remains a kind of ghost town: the sounds of joy and sadness, family sounds of birth and death and daily living, and the whine of machinery may still drift in the wind on quiet nights.

The self-guiding nature trail along the stream opposite Section B is a rewarding half-hour walk. A descriptive folder at the trailhead will guide you through the re-born forest and acquaint you with its intimate treasures. You don't have to camp here to enjoy the trail, nor to share in campground programs scheduled evenings in summer.

Left:
Smokemont
Campground

Right, from top:
Flume at Mingus
Mill; Mingus Mill; a
miller fills his sack
with meal in the
1940s.

Defacing historic structures in the park is against the law and is punishable by fines of up to $5,000 and six months in prison.

● MILE POST 29.9
MINGUS MILL

A short walk from the parking area is a working mill, built by the descendants of John Jacob Mingus in 1886 to replace his original mill built in the early 1800s.

Mingus Mill is one of two regularly operating grain mills in the park (the other is in Cades Cove) where you can still see corn being ground into meal from mid-March through November. Dr. Mingus, a physician, was a settler who served a growing population from this spot, built a reputation for honesty and good work, and prospered. He would also become a partner in the Alum

Cave Bluffs mining operation, discussed elsewhere in this guide. Mt. Mingus, just across Newfound Gap, bears his family name.

Millstones for corn, like the one used here, were huge local rocks chiseled round, flattened, and scored on the bottom to feed the meal out as kernels were ground. Wheat for flour required a much finer grind and stones for that task had to be imported, usually from France.

Mills were as vital to community life in those days as were water and land for farming. Grain would grow, but it had to be ground to provide the daily bread. The importance, and the evolution, of that humble machinery is graphically demonstrated here in the park.

Families often built small "tub mills," powered by water and providing grinding capacity for a family, plus maybe a neighbor or two. (A tub mill is preserved at the Alfred Reagan farm on the Roaring Fork Motor Nature Trail.)

Large water-driven mills (like this one and that at Cable Mill in Cades Cove) served large areas, and farmers brought their grain from miles around to be ground into meal and flour. Water-powered turbines, like this one at Mingus Mill, were a technological advance. A leaflet interpreting the mill, bags of stone-ground cornmeal and wheat flour, and other products and publications are available inside.

Talk to the millers here at Mingus Mill, and don't be shy about asking questions. They're preserving a lost art, and are happy to share the story of the mill's importance to mountain life.

● MILE POST 30.3
OCONALUFTEE VISITOR CENTER & MOUNTAIN FARM MUSEUM

The land doesn't need people, but people need the land. So the park tells two stories at once: the land and its people. The Mountain Farm Museum adjacent to the Oconaluftee Visitor Center tells the "people" story better than a hundred books. Your visit would be incomplete without a stop and stroll through here.

The visitor center is the place to learn what the park has to offer; places to see, things to do, special events, and numerous publications and exhibits which can make your trip more meaningful.

After visiting the center, take time to walk through the farm museum. While its buildings are authentic, they have been assembled here from scattered places in the park and combined to create an open-air

museum. A self-guiding booklet will tell you about the museum and its life. From spring through fall you may also see people representing the family and farmhands who worked on places like this, all dressed for the period they represent to help your imagination recreate a living heritage. Pigs,

chickens, horses, rows of heirloom vegetables, sorghum cane, and Hickory King corn further flesh out the scene.

By mountain standards, this could have been a successful place for a farm; rich bottomland for crops and livestock, good water supply, well-made buildings, even a productive sorghum cane mill.

Keep in mind as you visit that life was hard, but it was also rewarding and often full of joy. Had you lived in a place like this, you wouldn't miss "modern conveniences" such as electricity, plumbing, and machinery. The comforts you had were the modern conveniences for that day. We call it "simple" life, but it had its own complexities and rewards. And hard work, daylight to dark, was an absolute necessity.

Most mountain folk were smart and resourceful people, imaginative and self-reliant. They had to be. We can learn much from their legacy.

Left, from top: The apple house at the Mountain Farm Museum adjacent to the Oconaluftee Visitor Center; black-eyed Susan

Right, from top: Kitchen of Davis-Queen house; Mountain Farm Museum livestock and heirloom gardens bring the past to life; paling fence and the Davis-Queen house

● MILE 31.1
BLUE RIDGE PARKWAY

The end of one road is the beginning of another. The Blue Ridge Parkway begins or ends at this point depending on your direction of travel. It winds along the spine of the Appalachian Mountains 469 scenic miles to Shenandoah National Park in Virginia. Like the Smokies, the Blue Ridge Parkway is managed by the National Park Service and is one of our nation's crown jewels. There are no stoplights, stripmalls, or traffic jams, but plenty of mountain views, waterfalls, and warblers. Happy travels!

Clingmans Dome Road

7 Miles
FROM NEWFOUND GAP
ROAD TO CLINGMANS
DOME PARKING AREA

– CLOSED IN WINTER –

This is the park's popular high road, a spectacular seven-mile drive from its junction with Newfound Gap Road just south of the gap to the parking area with access to the highest point in the Smokies, 6,643 feet above sea level.

Views are outstanding—weather permitting—all along the route, and the observation tower atop the dome provides a magnificent panorama. The road offers many pullouts and overlooks, and features several short walks into the Appalachian high country. Your experience at this altitude looks and feels quite different from any other in the park. Don't be surprised if mist obscures your views. This is a world of plentiful moisture—that's what makes the Smokies special, after all—and clouds and fog are not unusual at this altitude.

As you look down these corrugated ridges and across the seamless carpet of forest, bear in mind that this is wild, rugged, and mostly trackless country. Don't be deceived by the relative ease with which you drive the roads or walk the trails. Would-be adventurers who wander from marked pathways run a real risk of getting quickly lost, falling down a rocky ravine, or worse.

The park's 270 miles of roads and 800 miles of footpaths cover a tiny percentage of its half-million acres. The rest of what you see is wilderness, preserved and protected, the most verdant in the country.

Left:
Spruce-fir forest at
Clingmans Dome

1
INDIAN GAP

This is a historic site, where two toll roads—one up each side of the mountain—met prior to the 1920s when Newfound Gap Road was built. The toll roads served a growing population of settlers and followed the well-used Indian route through here.

Indian Gap was long believed to be the lowest accessible crossing point in the heart of the mountains (until the "new-found" gap east of here was measured)—much shorter, for all its rough passage, than alternatives around the rugged peaks.

Pioneers followed the old Indian trail, hacking clearance wide enough in the 1830s to permit wagons to cross, and to drive cattle and hogs to market. In the years since it was abandoned, the forest has gradually reclaimed the old roadway.

Stop and walk a bit down the hill. You can still pick out the route and see the wagon

ruts. Looking down the rugged slope you can appreciate the enormous task faced by pioneers with hand tools cutting and maintaining this vital mountain crossing.

The trail continues for 3.3 miles down to the Chimney Tops parking area on Newfound Gap Road. It's a splendid walk through peaceful woods and along a rollicking little stream. Not bad going downhill. Should you take this hike, arrange for someone to meet you at the other end; climbing back up from the other end is demanding exercise.

2
THE FRASER FIR

You may notice the skeletal remains of fir trees in the forest around you. That's a tragedy of the southern Appalachians, comparable to the blight that wiped out the American chestnut trees early in the 20th century.

Here and elsewhere in the Appalachian high country, as in other parts of North America, firs are being attacked by the balsam woolly adelgid, which leaves devastation in its wake. This insect is non-native (exotic) to the Smokies and the United States, having been introduced from Europe. Trees can be individually treated (a limited number are, near the Balsam Mountain area) but what little hope there is probably lies in the possibility that a few Fraser firs may have a natural resistance to the adelgid.

Trees in these higher elevations also appear to be under attack from the pollutants carried in the air. Both acid rain and ground level ozone (smog) are known to harm plants, especially along the higher ridges. Unless a solution is found and pollution curtailed, vast portions of these splendid high forests will be changed forever.

Left, from top:
A family crosses the mountains through Indian Gap, circa 1911; Indian Gap Trail today.

● 3
CLINGMANS DOME

Right:
Fraser firs killed by balsam woolly adelgids

General Thomas Clingman was a colorful Civil War general, a North Carolina senator, and an energetic supporter of this region's great natural beauty a century before the movement to create a national park. Arnold Guyot, the intrepid Swiss geographer, named this highest peak in the Smokies in his honor.

This is the third highest mountain east of the Mississippi (Mt. Mitchell and Mt. Craig, 70 miles west in Yancey County, North Carolina, are both slightly higher). From the parking area a strenuous half-mile climb leads to a sloping ramp up to the observation tower at the summit.

CLINGMANS DOME,
ELEVATION 6,643'

Benches are provided along the trail, and you're advised to use them. At this altitude the air is a bit thinner (less oxygen), and the deceptively steep climb is more of a strain than you might expect.

An interesting phenomenon about Clingmans Dome: no matter how many times you make the trip to the top, the experience seems brand new. Seasons, of course, make a big difference. But so does the time of day, the way the sun's angle strikes the deeply rumpled landscape below you—never more impressive than at sunset. And the weather creates its own moods. There could be a cloudless view to an endless horizon, or sometimes an eerie sense of isolation as the rolling fog creates a brooding, surrealistic scene. Or clouds may linger far below, obscuring the lowlands to leave deep green islands floating on a dreamy sea.

Left, from top:
Clingmans Dome
observation tower;
Spring-beauty

Right:
Catawba
rhododendron
bloom in the spruce-
fir forest

4
WEEPING WALL

Moisture is critical to abundant life in the Smokies at all altitudes. Even here atop the mountain you can see, among exposed rock faces along the road, water seeping constantly in drips, rivulets, or small waterfalls. In winter these "weeping walls" create strange ice sculptures, massive white columns, and unusual "iceballs" where the water plops and freezes. In warmer weather the moisture adds its patina to the character of the ancient rock,

CLINGMANS DOME

Named for Brigadier General Thomas Lanier Clingman (1812-1897), soldier, mining expert, explorer, antebellum political leader, scientist, and all-around colorful character. He was the first man to accurately measure the height of his namesake peak in the 1850s. He was a staunch leader in the North Carolina Whig political party and, when the Civil War broke out, he joined the Confederacy.

He was often described as a vain, conceited, but scholarly and brave man, who never married; he died impoverished in the state mental hospital.

Clingmans Dome is the highest peak in the park and the highest elevation in the state of Tennessee. Seven states are said to be visible from the observation tower on a clear day.

feeding the moss and fern that find their foothold there.

Little springs like these give rise to rushing streams, and ultimately nourish great rivers—the Tennessee, Ohio, and Mississippi. The rainfall at this altitude is even more abundant than that down below, where more than 50 inches per year are measured. Here, up to 85 inches annually help insure that life is sustained, and great rivers are fed.

Not far down the slope before you are the modest trickles that unite into Deep Creek, the Tuckasegee River, Fontana Lake, and the Little Tennessee River. Just across the ridge opposite, similar springs give rise to the turbulent Little River, flowing on through Elkmont and out of the park to join the Tennessee.

● 5

SPRUCE-FIR NATURE TRAIL

Here's a real treat, a venture into the distinctive world of the high Smokies. It's a half-mile round trip, easy walking, and a rare experience. A self-guiding leaflet at the trail's start will acquaint you with life at this altitude, and point out little wonders you might otherwise miss.

Sights, sounds—even smells—are different here. Take a lung-full of the cool, fir-scented mountain air. Watch for the darting bird— maybe a Black-capped Chickadee or the Red-breasted Nuthatch—among the evergreens. Notice those strange trees with stilted roots lifting their trunks above the ground. They grew that way around "nurse" or "mother" trees, decaying logs that nourished new life.

Most of all, listen. A very special stillness pervades the high country.

Little River Road

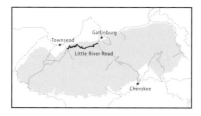

This 18-mile drive between Sugarlands Visitor Center and the park entrance at Townsend, Tennessee, offers a low-elevation streamside drive through the Smokies. Little River Road—which also leads to Cades Cove—is second only to the over-mountain Newfound Gap Road in popularity among motorists.

It's an easy drive, with no mountains to climb. But twisting its way through the river's gorge, it demands that you drive slowly and exercise special care on curves and at pullouts.

Stops are numbered in sequence from Sugarlands Visitor Center westward. If you are driving from the west, follow the markers in reverse order.

Between the Elkmont turnoff and Townsend, the road follows the sinuous turbulence of Little River through leafy tunnels, the roar of the river on one hand and silent rock walls on the other. It's a beautiful drive through the ancient gorge, with plenty of stopping places—marked and unmarked—along your route. Pause to poke about on your own, and get acquainted with the many faces of Little River.

Left:
Little River

Right:
Little River Road

The river is capricious. Here the water is placid, crystal clear, almost motionless. There it changes suddenly into a rush of whitewater tumbling around huge rocks with roar and froth. Enjoy the water, but please use good sense about it. Changes in current can be treacherous; the water is colder than you think; and depths (as much as 15 feet) are often greater than they appear.

● 1
MALONEY POINT

**MALONEY POINT,
ELEVATION 2,120'**

This overlook honors the memory of General Frank Maloney of Knoxville, an early park advocate who helped determine its ultimate boundaries. From here you're looking back down the course of Fighting Creek toward Gatlinburg and Webb Mountain beyond. "Fighting Creek" sounds as though it recalls some historic battle, or maybe the turbulence of the stream, but the name's origin is more mundane than romantic. It was the disputed location of a school in the 19th century.

Across the low gap at the turnoff to Elkmont the road joins the course of the Little River, which runs west. Fighting Creek flows due east. Both wind up north of here—an oddity of mountain terrain—nourishing the Tennessee River.

● 2
LAUREL FALLS TRAIL

The parking areas for this popular short hike are on both sides of the road, so watch for cars and people. One of the prettiest of the park's many waterfalls, Laurel Falls is fortunately easy to reach and worth the extra hour or so. A paved trail leads all the way through cool, quiet woods—a pleasant 2.5-mile round trip.

You'll find a descriptive leaflet at the trailhead to point out highlights along the

*Left:
A photographer
focuses his camera
on a vista from
Maloney Point.*

*Right, from top:
Laurel Falls; visitors
hike up Laurel Falls
Trail.*

MALONEY POINT

Named for General Frank Maloney (1879-1952). In addition to helping establish the boundaries of the park, he also proposed the route of the Blue Ridge Parkway in North Carolina and conceived the idea of the Foothills Parkway in Tennessee. He selected the route for the parkway, a 72-mile-long scenic highway, and shepherded the state and federal legislation necessary for its development. For this reason, he is known as the Father of the Foothills Parkway.

way. If you like to add a touch of adventure, continue on the more rugged trail past the falls for a half mile to enter a splendid stand of virgin hardwoods.

● 3

ELKMONT CAMPGROUND & NATURE TRAIL

Once a logging camp and vacation community with scores of summer cottages, Elkmont is now a well-developed park campground. Whether staying here or not, you're welcome to enjoy the walks and talks given by park rangers and volunteers. Schedules are posted on the campground bulletin boards.

On the way up the 1.5-mile drive to the campground you pass the site of the old Wonderland Hotel on your left. This rustic resort, no longer in operation, is a vestige of Elkmont's heyday as a vacation playground early in the 20th century.

A road across from the campground entrance leads to the parking area for the

Vehicle break-ins sometimes occur at trailheads. Lock your car and keep purses, cameras, portable stereos, and other valuables on your person or lock them in the trunk before you get to the trailhead.

Elkmont self-guiding nature trail and a good lesson in learning to read the natural history that surrounds you. The trail is a short excursion of less than a mile, through land that has been much used by humans for a century or more and is now returning to its primal state. Once heavily logged, the land bears traces of railroad spurs now obscured by new growth. A descriptive leaflet is available at the trailhead.

About a quarter-mile beyond the nature trail the road forks. The left fork becomes Little River Trail, a relatively easy route that follows its scenic namesake for 6.2 miles. The right fork of the road allows access to Jakes Creek trailhead and an area of old summer cottages.

Left, from top: Camping in the Smokies; a quiet section of Little River; the Wonderland Hotel in the 1930s—note the train tracks running in front at the base of the hill. This old rail bed is where the road is today.

● 4
METCALF BOTTOMS PICNIC AREA & LITTLE GREENBRIER SCHOOL

This excellent picnic area is named for the family who farmed the rich bottomland along the river long before the park was here. There's plenty of parking and many shady picnic tables in the cozy woods and along the river.

The road over the wooden bridge here at Metcalf Bottoms leads to a lovely vestige of "life in the old days." Cross the bridge and take the first right onto a narrow gravel road (closed in winter). It's about a mile up this pretty forest road to Little Greenbrier School and cemetery. This rustic building was at the heart of Little Greenbrier, a pre-park community scattered around Metcalf Bottoms. (There was also a Big Greenbrier, on the Little Pigeon's Middle Prong several miles east of Gatlinburg.)

Built of split logs up to two feet wide, this building was used as a community school and church from 1882 until 1936, when the land became part of the park. Original benches and desks are still there, along with a lectern and painted blackboard.

Adjacent to the building and surrounded by weathered pickets is a small, poignant

HISTORIC PRESERVATION

The park contains more than 100 historic buildings, including the finest and most complete collection of southern Appalachian log cabins, barns, and related outbuildings. Most range in time from the 1830s Euro-American settlement to the early twentieth century. National Park Service staff work diligently to preserve these reminders of our past to help teach future generations about southern Appalachian culture.

The all-too-common practice of writing one's name on historic structures is a major threat to preservation. Vandalism degrades the integrity of historic buildings and mars the beauty of their craftsmanship. Each time graffiti has to be removed, some of the building's original fabric is lost and part of our history turns to sawdust.

Help support the preservation efforts of the park! Please refrain from writing or carving on these structures and notify a park ranger when you see vandalism taking place.

Defacing historic structures in the park is against the law and is punishable by fines of up to $5,000 and six months in prison.

cemetery; many of its graves are those of children. Original fieldstone markers are still in place, though small marble headstones have been added to some.

The Walker Sisters' farmstead is about one mile past the gated road. John Walker settled in Little Greenbrier after the Civil War and reared his 11 children here. Five of his daughters, all unmarried, kept the old homestead after their father's death and continued to live here even after the park's creation. The self-reliant and eminently hospitable Walker Sisters became an attraction in themselves, sharing their lifestyle and their lore with many visitors until 1964, when Louisa, the youngest surviving daughter, died at age 82.

About a mile past the turnoff to the school is the park boundary. From here the road descends into beautiful Wear Cove. If you follow the paved road to your right along Cove Creek you will rejoin U.S. Highway 441 at Pigeon Forge. A left turn will take you along U.S. 321 to Townsend. Some travelers use this route as a convenient alternative entrance to or shortcut exit from this part of the park.

● 5

THE SINKS

Rising from springs and branches 6,000 feet up on the face of Clingmans Dome, Little River tumbles down through Elkmont and cuts its way here through a deepening gorge with vigorous beauty all the way. At The Sinks, it confronts a hard rock wall and turns sharply with a great roar to pour between giant rocks in a violent cascade. The

constant force of all that water has cut deep pools into the rock, creating a handsome spot to stop and sense, more than anywhere else, the power of the rushing river.

The old riverbed, hidden in vegetation, was abandoned as the river sought softer rock and shifted its course. Eventually, many centuries from now, the water will cut its way back further still and relocate these whitewater falls.

The area is congested with people and vehicles, so be extra cautious. Also be cautious around the slippery rocks beside the falls. The small parking area is limited and restricted, so there may be times when stopping here is difficult.

● 6

MEIGS FALLS

This is one of the few waterfalls visible from a road in the Great Smokies, and under the right conditions it is a glorious sight to behold. Unlike The Sinks, Meigs Falls is not a drop of Little River proper, but of tributary Meigs Creek.

It's easy to miss this waterfall on the far side of Little River, so watch carefully for a large parking area on the river side of the road. Trees partially obscure the falls in summer, making late fall and winter some of the best times to photograph and enjoy it. After wet weather, Meigs Falls is truly impressive.

Meigs Creek pours down from Meigs Mountain above. Both are named for Return Jonathan Meigs who surveyed the area in the early 1800s. Mr. Meigs' unusual given name is said to come from a turning point in the courtship of his mother and father. The senior

Meigs was in the process of riding away from his beloved, perhaps forever, when she halted his retreat with "Return, Jonathan, return!" The word was such beautiful music to Mr. Meigs' ears, he decided to so name his son.

A remarkable, perhaps one-of-a-kind, piece of logging era engineering stood just east of

the falls in the early 1920s—a swinging railroad bridge across Little River. The bridge solved the problem of getting a whole lot of logs across Little River from the rugged Meigs Creek drainage.

Like a swinging footbridge, the railroad bridge had no intermediate supports and so hung low and loose between ends. Rail cars loaded with Meigs Creek drainage logs were carefully lowered across the bridge with cables and a big steam engine. The emptied cars were likewise retrieved.

● 7

TOWNSEND "Y"

The Middle and Left prongs join the Little River here where the roads fork, a mile from the park boundary at Townsend. The streams' wide union is a much-enjoyed playground—a broad and peaceful stretch of river with good spots for wading or sunning. It's usually congested, so be alert for cars and people.

And do take note of the sign on the bank

Left, from top: Meigs Falls; A swinging railroad bridge across Little River at the mouth of Meigs Creek, circa 1918. An incline steam engine had a drum with a coil of steel cable. Loggers would take the end of the cable and loop it around a large stump on the top of the hill. The engineer on the engine would then start the drum, the cable would wind, and the train cars were drawn up or lowered down the bridge.

warning of river hazards; many serious accidents occur in the water. Tubing, for all its frolicking good time, can be especially dangerous. This particular spot is wide and tranquil (but watch those rocks). Not far away, upstream in the gorge, hidden currents and surprising depths can catch you unaware. Fatalities have occurred. Quiet water can abruptly become a torrent; rocks are many, often hidden, and slippery. An unprotected child riding an inner tube, without steering or rudder, is at the mercy of the current.

At this point on the road, you're one mile from Townsend, seven miles from Cades Cove, and 17.5 miles from Sugarlands Visitor Center.

QUIET WALKWAYS

Boyd Evison served as superintendent at Great Smoky Mountains National Park from 1975-78. He is noted for having created the park's system of short, easy walking trails known as "quiet walkways," which offer visitors a chance to get out of their vehicles and into the environment for at least a brief experience.

Evison is considered to be one of the greatest and most influential leaders of the modern National Park Service. His career was dedicated to conservation, environmental education, and courageous leadership in the field of natural resource protection. He touched the lives of thousands of National Park Service employees and influenced the overall management of the entire national park system and its service to 280 million annual visitors.

Bears: Guidelines for your Safety

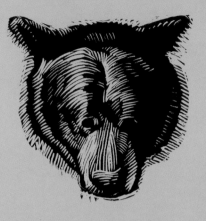

Great Smoky Mountains National Park is one of the few places remaining in the eastern United States where black bears can live in wild, natural surroundings.

Bears inhabit all elevations of the park. Though populations are variable, recent estimates state that approximately 1,500 bears live in the park. This equals a population density of approximately two bears per square mile.

Bears in the park are wild and their behavior is sometimes unpredictable. *Although extremely rare, attacks on humans have occurred, inflicting serious injuries and death.* Treat bear encounters with extreme caution and follow these guidelines:

• If you see a bear remain watchful. *Do not approach it.* If your presence causes the bear to change its behavior (stops feeding, changes its travel direction, watches you, etc.)—you're too close. Being too close may provoke aggressive behavior from the bear such as running toward you, making loud noises, or swatting the ground. The bear is demanding more space.

• If a bear persistently follows or approaches you, without vocalizing, or paw swatting, try changing your direction. If the bear continues to follow you, stand your

ground. If the bear gets closer, talk loudly or shout at it. Act aggressively and try to intimidate the bear. Act together as a group if you have companions. Make yourselves look as large as possible (for example, move to higher ground). Throw non-food objects such as rocks at the bear. Use a deterrent such as a stout stick. *Don't run*, but slowly back away, watching the bear. Try to increase the distance between you and the bear. The bear will probably do the same. If a bear physically attacks you, fight back aggressively with any available object—the bear might consider you prey! Above all, keep your distance from bears! *Don't leave food for the bear*; this encourages further problems.

The bear's keen sense of smell leads it to nuts and berries, but the animal is also enticed by human food left on a picnic table or offered from an outstretched hand. Feeding bears or allowing them access to human food causes a number of problems:

• It changes the bear's wild behavior and causes them to lose their instinctive fear of humans. This lack of fear causes panhandler or "nuisance" bears to be more unpredictable and dangerous when they encounter humans.

• It transforms wild and healthy bears into habitual beggars. Panhandler bears damage property and injure people. Habitual panhandler bears must be adversely conditioned or destroyed.

Studies also show that panhandler bears never live as long as wild bears. Many are hit by cars and become easy targets for poachers. Beggar

bears may die from ingesting food packaging. Many bears have died a slow and agonizing death from eating plastics and other materials. *Garbage Kills Bears!*

National Park Rangers issue citations for wildlife harassment, feeding bears, and improper food storage, which is punishable by fines of up to $5,000 and/or imprisonment of up to six months. Visitors are urged to view all wildlife at a safe distance and to never leave food or garbage unattended.

Help protect others. Report all bear incidents to a park ranger immediately or call (865) 436-1230.

Laurel Creek Road

Laurel Creek Road is a winding, scenic, seven-mile drive leading to one of the park's most interesting attractions, Cades Cove.

The Laurel Creek Road that leads to the cove is an attraction in itself. Many pullovers are provided as the road meanders along the tumbling creek, through the refreshing lowland forest, and over Crib Gap.

An interesting side trip is the winding drive up the Tremont Road. This road follows the lovely Middle Prong of Little River to the Great Smoky Mountains Institute at Tremont. The Institute provides environmental education programs for everyone from school groups to Elderhostels. A small visitor center there offers information and publications about the park.

A gravel road (closed in winter) continues for three miles beyond the Institute. A self-guiding auto tour booklet, available from a box on the roadside, details the area's fascinating logging history.

Left:
Middle Prong of
Little Pigeon River
near Tremont

Right, from top:
Tunnel on Laurel
Creek Road; Laurel
Creek

Cades Cove Loop Road

Euro-American settlement of Cades Cove began in the early 1800s, and at its peak the beautiful cove was home to 700 people, with scores of homes, stores, and other buildings. When it became part of the park in the 1930s, initial plans were to allow the area to be reclaimed by the wilderness. In wise reconsideration, park officials agreed that human history is a vital chapter in the Smokies story, and should be preserved.

Most of the original buildings are gone. Those that remain are a living tribute to those people whose home this was. For more than a century theirs was a thriving settlement, pleasantly secluded but quite in touch with the outside world as well.

Several homes and churches are preserved as tangible examples of life in another time. The John Cable Mill, still grinding corn with its giant water-powered millstone,

Left:
Cades Cove

Right:
A doe and fawn

is a highlight of the tour. Stone-ground meal is available when the mill is operating from mid-March through November.

The Cades Cove tour is a paved, 11-mile, one-way loop that returns you to its starting point.

The cove offers amenities for the modern visitor, including a popular campground and picnic area at the start of the loop. Rental bicycles are also available seasonally here for alternative transportation around the cove. A small visitor center, open every day but Christmas, is adjacent to the Cable Mill and features exhibits of early life in the Smokies.

The loop itself is closed at dusk and during periods of high water or adverse winter weather. Traffic can be extremely heavy during the season and on weekends throughout the year. Driving time may be three hours during busy times. However, short cuts using Sparks or Hyatt lanes are available if you're in a hurry.

Two short but highly rewarding roads exit the park from the Cades Cove loop: Rich Mountain and Parson Branch. Details on each are given elsewhere in this road guide.

Quite aside from its human legacy, Cades Cove is a splendid scenic attraction and something of a natural wonder. It's five miles long, less than two miles wide, and almost perfectly flat (at about 1,750 feet above sea level). The auto-tour loop skirts the cleared lowland and Cades Cove is completely surrounded by majestic mountains.

Photo opportunities are many. Deer, bear, groundhogs, coyotes, and even occasional Wild Turkeys are not uncommon along the road, especially in early morning and late afternoon.

According to lore, the name "Cades" Cove comes from Cherokee chief Cade (or Kade) who once considered the cove as part of his domain. The creek that flows through the cove bears the name of the great Cherokee chief Abram, as do the beautiful falls that await the hiker 2.5 miles from the loop road.

Defacing historic structures in the park is against the law and is punishable by fines of up to $5,000 and six months in prison.

1
BEGIN ONE-WAY

When Cades Cove was a farming community, an unpaved two-way road followed the same general route as the present 11-mile one-way loop road. The orientation shelter on your left is often staffed with rangers or volunteers who can answer your questions about the road ahead.

Left, from top:
Cades Cove Loop
Road borders fields
of grasses and
wildflowers

Right:
Sparks Lane in
Cades Cove; John
Oliver cabin

2
SPARKS LANE

This two-way, north-south road connects at each end with the loop road. It has been part of the cove road system since the 1840s. If you need to return to the campground or to leave the cove, take this shortcut to the eastbound arm of the Cades Cove Loop Road.

3
JOHN OLIVER PLACE

This is one of over 100 historic buildings in the park. The collection of log structures is believed to be the largest of its kind in the East. John Oliver arrived in the cove prior to 1820 and received title for this land in 1826. It remained in the family until the park was established more than 100 years later. Large families often lived in such small buildings. Exact arrangements differed from family to family. Usually, however, parents, infants and daughters slept on the first floor and sons slept in the loft. Not much except mules, muscles, simple tools and neighborly help was needed to fell the trees, get them to the building site and build the house. The notched corners need no nails or pegs; gravity holds them together. Chinks (open spaces between logs) were filled with mud to seal out wind, snow and rain. The stone chimney is held together with mud mortar.

Left, from top:
Primitive Baptist
Church; Swallowtail
butterfly; Cades
Cove fields viewed
from Loop Road

Right, from top:
Tombstone in
cemetery at
Methodist Church;
Missionary Baptist
Church; Hyatt Lane

● **4**

PRIMITIVE BAPTIST CHURCH

Some of the earliest Euro-American settlers established this church in 1827. A log building served their needs until this one replaced it in 1887. The church closed during the Civil War. Official church correspondence after the war explained it all: "We the Primitive Baptist Church in Blount County in Cades Cove, do show the public why we have not kept up our church meeting. It was on account of the Rebellion and we was Union people and the Rebels was too strong here in Cades Cove. Our preacher was obliged to leave sometimes, and thank God we once more can meet." Some of the early settlers lie in the cemetery. The Consolidated School stood to the left of the road leading to the church.

● **5**

METHODIST CHURCH

J.D. McCampbell, a blacksmith and carpenter, built this church in 115 days for $115. He later served many years as its minister. Methodists were not as numerous as Baptists in the cove, but enough of them got together in the 1820s to establish the church in a log building that lasted until this one replaced it in 1902. The Civil War and Reconstruction divided the church,

as they did other Methodist congregations. Dissidents formed the Hopewell Methodist Church on the opposite side of the cove. It no longer stands. Notice that the church has two front doors. This usually indicates the church follows the custom of men sitting on one side of the house and women on the other. But this church didn't follow that custom. The two doors are there because the church borrowed the building plans of another church that did divide its congregation by gender.

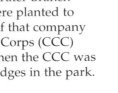

6
HYATT LANE

Once part of a Cherokee trail, this two-way road across the cove later served residents and now is used by visitors who want either to cut short their tour of the cove or to repeat the western portion of it. Plots of tall native grasses and wildflowers grow near a section of the road.

7
MISSIONARY BAPTIST CHURCH

A group of Baptists expelled from the Primitive Baptist Church because they favored missionary work formed this church in 1839. The church ceased to meet during the Civil War. It resumed activity after the war but without members who had been Confederate sympathizers. This building dates from 1915. A Sunday school started in the church in 1898 continued until the church closed in 1944. During March and into April, look for daffodils on the right between the church and the Tater Branch crossing. Notice that they were planted to read, "Co. 5427." Members of that company of the Civilian Conservation Corps (CCC) planted them in the 1930s when the CCC was building trails, roads and bridges in the park.

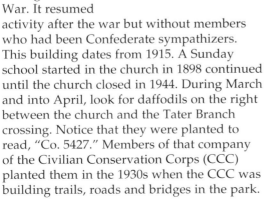

● 8
RICH MOUNTAIN ROAD

Motorists may leave the cove and the park by this route but they cannot enter by it. The road is closed in winter. See complete description ahead in this guide.

● 9
COOPER ROAD TRAIL

Now a pleasant hiking trail, much of the Cooper Road Trail first was part of an Indian trail. Daniel David Foute, a big property owner in the cove, laid it out in the 1830s as part of a route to Maryville. In the 1840s Joe Cooper improved it to wagon road status. It was the most direct route to Maryville for people in the western end of the cove.

● 10
ELIJAH OLIVER PLACE

Elijah Oliver, son of John Oliver, whose cabin you saw earlier, was born in the cove in 1824. After he married, he and his family moved out of the cove before the Civil War. After the war, he bought this property and moved back in. In that time and place, more buildings were required for living than now. With no refrigerator or freezer, they needed the springhouse to keep milk and butter cool. They needed the smokehouse to store and preserve hams, shoulders and side meat for an entire year. They ate mostly pork because it was easier to preserve than other meats. They needed the corncrib to store enough corn for grinding into meal to last until the next harvest. Having no automobile or motorized farm equipment, they needed horses or mules to pull plows, harrows, buggies, sleds and wagons. And they needed a barn to shelter these animals, along with the cows that provided milk. Hay to feed them was stored in the barn loft. Water for drinking, cooking, bathing, and laundry had to be carried from the spring. No easy task.

Left, from top:
Moonlight shines down on Cades Cove

Right, from top:
Cable Mill's famous water-wheel; miller at Cable Mill

● 11
CABLE MILL HISTORIC AREA

Be sure and stop here, and not only because you'll find the only restrooms along the loop. There's lots to see and do. The visitor center (open every day but Christmas)

offers a history exhibit, information, and lots of wares for sale—books, maps, music, toys, and old-time foods. Cable Mill is an operating water-powered gristmill with a postcard perfect overshot waterwheel, just like in the storybooks. The mill operates from 9 a.m. to 5 p.m. from mid-March through November. Rangers and volunteers lead tours of the area during the season. An inexpensive booklet containing a walking tour of the Cable Mill historic area is available at the visitor center. Other area highlights include a cantilever barn, a furnished 1879 home, a blacksmith shop, and a smokehouse.

● 12
HENRY WHITEHEAD PLACE

Matilda Shields Gregory's husband deserted her and their small son. In the emergency, her brothers hastily built this small log cabin for them. Henry Whitehead's wife died, leaving him with three daughters to rear. Henry courted and married Matilda. He built for them this larger house of square-sawed logs. The log sections are four inches thick, enough to provide plenty of insulation. At first glance, the building looks like a frame house—until you notice the jointed corners. Some call it a "transition" house, a link between regular log houses and frame houses built of sawed lumber. It was one of three such houses in Cades Cove and it is the only one left in the park.

**CADES COVE
VISITOR CENTER,
ELEVATION 1,716'**

Sawed log houses were not built until sawmills came to the cove. This pair of buildings represents the roughest and finest of log construction in the Smokies.

● **13**
CADES COVE NATURE TRAIL

This is a dry type forest where pines and oaks predominate.

Chestnuts once grew here and you may see sprouts growing from the chestnut root systems that still live. You also may see red maples, dogwoods, and sourwoods. In July sourwood blooms provide nectar for the region's prized sourwood honey. Early settlers used the crooked trunks of sourwoods to make sled runners. Sourwood leaves take on a lovely red hue in autumn.

● **14**
HYATT LANE

If you wish to have another look at something in the western end of the cove, turn here and follow this road back to the westbound leg of the loop road.

● **15**
DAN LAWSON PLACE

Dan Lawson built this house in 1856, on land bought from his father-in-law, Peter Cable, whose home stood to the west across the stream. The brick chimney, unusual for the time and locale, was built of bricks made on the site. Lawson owned a swath of land starting at the Tennessee-North Carolina line on the mountain crest to the south and coming down the mountain and across the cove and north to the top of Cades Cove Mountain. The original house of hewn logs was built before sawmills came to the cove, but an examination shows that sawed lumber later was used in additions and maintenance. The small building closest to the house is a granary; the other is a smokehouse.

● **16**
TIPTON PLACE

"Colonel Hamp" Tipton, who served in the Mexican War, owned property in Cades Cove but lived in Tuckaleechee Cove. He had this house built in the early 1870s. Among those who lived in it were his daughters,

Left:
The day's last light
shines down on
Cades Cove

Right, from top:
Tipton house; Sweet
white trillium
mingles with
columbine; Carter
Shields cabin

"Miss Lucy" and "Miss Lizzie," who taught school in the cove, and the James McCaulley family. The McCaulleys rented the place briefly in the late 1870s before James bought land and built his own home, plus blacksmith and carpentry shops. The blacksmith shop James used here stands nearby in the hollow. The long shed on the opposite side of the house sheltered bee gums. A smokehouse and a woodshed are in the front yard. On the other side of the road stands a double-pen corn crib and a cantilever barn, a replica of an earlier one in the same place.

● 17
CARTER SHIELDS CABIN

A wound suffered in the Civil War Battle of Shiloh left George Washington "Carter" Shields crippled for life. Shortly after the war he married and moved to Kansas. He returned to Cades Cove in 1906 and bought this property in 1910. One would think that an old soldier could find contentment in such a lovely nook. But Shields lived here only 11 years before leaving again.

● 18
SPARKS LANE

This two-way road is named for a widely known Cades Cove family. Three Sparks brothers, Tom, Dave, and Sam, were livestock herders in the high Smokies during the summer months. Your tour is nearly ended—unless you wish to turn left on Sparks Lane and repeat most of it.

Rich Mountain Road

– CLOSED IN WINTER –

Here's one of the less-traveled roads that can make a difference in your park experience. It's a historic route, traveled since the 1830s, and well used by Indians for many generations before that.

It begins on the Cades Cove loop directly across from the Missionary Baptist Church and is identified as post number 8. The road climbs Rich Mountain for seven miles to the park boundary, then descends into Tuckaleechee Cove and some very pretty countryside outside the park for five more miles into Townsend.

The sign at its start calls it "primitive," but by mountain standards it's a good country road— amply wide, well graded with a good gravel surface, one-way traffic to the park boundary. Motor homes, buses, vans longer than 15 feet, and trailers are prohibited.

Highlights are outstanding views of Cades Cove and the park on one side of the mountain, and of Tuckaleechee Cove on the other. Plus, of course, the intimate uncrowded acquaintance with the mountains that you won't find on busier routes. Use a lower gear when going downhill for less wear on your brakes. Speed limits are posted, but the signs are superfluous: 15 mph is about tops.

You won't find better views of the cove—or, for that matter the mainline of the Great Smokies towering beyond—than the first clearing about a mile up the mountain.

STOP

MOTOR HOMES,
BUSES, VANS
LONGER THAN 15
FEET, AND
TRAILERS ARE
PROHIBITED!

Left:
Driving Rich
Mountain Road on
an early fall day

Right:
The Methodist
church in Cades
Cove as seen from
Rich Mountain Road

A couple of miles farther on is an even more dramatic view of the park (though the cove is hidden by the terrain at this point).

There's no gap at the top in the usual sense. Instead, the mountain seems to level out for easy passage at 2,600 feet. As the road descends toward Tuckaleechee there are fine views of this other lovely cove just outside the park.

The "road over Rich Mountain" was nothing more than an Indian trail somewhere in the dim past, then became the first major route into Cades Cove for settlers in the early 1800s. At a few places along the modern route, you may still spot the old roadbed meandering from the present road in the woods here and there.

This makes a good "undiscovered" drive any time, as well as an alternative route from Cades Cove. The road is closed in winter, but no time is better than the fall, when the red-and-gold glory of the mountains surrounds you entirely and there's new beauty at every turn.

Left, from top: Rich Mountain Road meandering through the forest above Cades Cove; Mountain gentian; a white-tailed buck pauses at the forest edge in Cades Cove.

Bird Checklist

- ❏ Broad-winged Hawk
- ❏ Turkey Vulture
- ❏ Mourning Dove
- ❏ Chimney Swift
- ❏ Ruby-throated Hummingbird
- ❏ Eastern Wood Pewee
- ❏ Acadian Flycatcher
- ❏ Eastern Phoebe
- ❏ Barn Swallow
- ❏ Blue-headed Vireo
- ❏ Yellow-throated Vireo
- ❏ Red-eyed Vireo
- ❏ Blue Jay
- ❏ American Crow
- ❏ Carolina Chickadee
- ❏ Tufted Titmouse
- ❏ Red-breasted Nuthatch
- ❏ Carolina Wren
- ❏ Winter Wren
- ❏ Golden-crowned Kinglet
- ❏ Blue-gray Gnatcatcher
- ❏ Veery
- ❏ Swainson's Thrush
- ❏ Wood Thrush
- ❏ American Robin
- ❏ European Starling
- ❏ Tennessee Warbler
- ❏ Chestnut-sided Warbler
- ❏ Magnolia Warbler
- ❏ Black-throated Blue Warbler

- ❏ Yellow-rumped Warbler
- ❏ Black-throated Green Warbler
- ❏ Black-and-white Warbler
- ❏ Ovenbird
- ❏ Louisiana Waterthrush
- ❏ Kentucky Warbler
- ❏ Hooded Warbler
- ❏ Canada Warbler
- ❏ Scarlet Tanager
- ❏ Eastern Towhee
- ❏ Chipping Sparrow
- ❏ Field Sparrow
- ❏ Song Sparrow
- ❏ White-throated Sparrow
- ❏ Dark-eyed Junco
- ❏ Northern Cardinal
- ❏ Indigo Bunting
- ❏ Red-winged Blackbird
- ❏ Eastern Meadowlark
- ❏ Pine Siskin
- ❏ Evening Grosbeak

Parson Branch Road

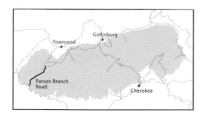

8 MILES
FROM FORGE CREEK ROAD
TO HIGHWAY 129

– CLOSED IN WINTER –

Nowhere else in the Smokies can you plunge into the primeval past from the comfort of a car quite as you do on Parson Branch Road. This eight-mile drive takes you through a towering forest along a graveled-over wagon track—the same route followed out of Cades Cove for 150 years.

Since this is a one-way drive leading out of the park, it can serve as a good loop tour by combining Parson Branch Road, a 10-mile drive along Chilhowee Lake at the park's perimeter, and the 17-mile west portion of the Foothills Parkway (discussed elsewhere in this guide). From the Foothills Parkway terminus, it's nine miles back to the park entrance at Townsend.

On Parson Branch Road, it's easy to sense how the area used to be as you climb and dip and turn among majestic hemlocks and tuliptrees four feet thick and more, their tops a canopy a hundred feet overhead. Your imagination can take away the gravel surface, replace your internal combustion engine with real horsepower, and vault you into another age. You'll return to a time long before the park and the tourists, when travelers cut passages to find the overmountain river and follow its course to distant, necessary places.

Parson Branch Road

Today, Parson Branch Road is never more than a few miles from pavement. A tough little road— narrow graveled bed with a few steep ups and downs, it's not for wide-bodies or high-top campers but poses no problem for cars and trucks. It brings a remote sense of wild splendor you won't forget.

About 1830, a toll road, Parson's Turnpike, was built around the west end of the Smokies, following the Little Tennessee (the present route of U.S. 129). To give cove residents access to the turnpike and an overmountain route into North Carolina, the branch road was authorized in 1838. Its supervisor was Russell Gregory, an early resident whose land included the area now called Gregory Bald.

Many small streams (among them Testament Branch and Bible Creek) rise on the flanks of Parson Bald, a mainline Smokies' knob with a natural clearing on top. Parsons gathered their flocks to brush-arbor revivals held in that high clearing in the early 1800s.

The road to Parson Branch turns off the Cades Cove loop just past the visitor center at Cable Mill. There to your right, past the Henry Whitehead Cabin, across the little bridge and through a tunnel of giant rhododendron, you'll encounter a fascinating Smokies experience.

Left:
Henry Whitehead place

Right, from top:
A Pileated Woodpecker feeds its young; a fawn hides in the overgrowth.

● 1
OVER THE TOP

After you've topped the steep rise, the road undulates through the lush woods. There are no precipitous slopes or rocky cliffs here, no sweeping vistas, only the stillness of the forest.

PARSON BRANCH

Named for Joshua Parson, an early settler in the area who lived near the confluence of Abrams Creek and the Little Tennessee River. He constructed the Parson's Turnpike along Little River, circa 1829. It may also have been named for religious revivals conducted here by ministers (or parsons) in the early 1800s.

A good place to stop, shut off the engine. Listen to the quiet. Feel the wonder of the wild. This seems a world away from the one you left not long ago, a vastly different time and place.

A mature forest now thrusts through the deep thickets of rhododendron that cover these well-watered slopes. Almost constant moisture from streams and rainfall and rising mists (the "smoke" of the Smokies) cloaks giant trunks with a patina of moss. Some huge trunks lie prone and will outlast many generations of humans. Slowly, but surely, they will decay and nourish the land that gave them life. In death as in life, the trees are vital to the cycle.

**HANNAH
MOUNTAIN,
ELEVATION 2,779'**

● 2

SAMS GAP

You're crossing Hannah Mountain. Abruptly the woods are different, but only for a while. This is a more open, somewhat drier hardwood forest that will be replaced farther on by more giant trees and more lush thickets of rhododendron, in a replay of the primal scene where you began.

As you came up from Cades Cove, your ascent was at first steep, followed by an up-and-down gradual climb across the mountain. Beyond this point, at least for a time, the descent is fairly steady and steep. For the sake of your brakes, a lower gear is recommended for the whole route, and at times even first gear can be used.

Hannah Mountain is a long ridge that joins the mainline Smokies at Gregory Bald about two miles southeast of here, and a ridgetop trail from here unites with the Appalachian Trail at that point.

Like all ridges, this serves as a small divide. As you drove up, streams flowed toward you; on your descent you'll follow other streams' downward rush toward the Little Tennessee River.

● 3
PANTHER CREEK

This little creek twists and tumbles its way westward from here to flow into Chilhowee Lake near the beginning of the Foothills Parkway, through the roadless and trailless wilderness at the west end of the park.

The stream is called Panther Creek, honoring the sleek and handsome predator once fairly common in the Smokies but now rarely reported. Panther, "painter," cougar, catamount—all are indigenous names given to the eastern mountain lion, largest of American cats. Occasional unofficial reports are received from hikers and others that some panthers may still roam these remote areas, but sightings haven't been confirmed. His smaller cousin the bobcat is a park denizen, though reclusive and rarely seen.

Left, from top:
Parson Branch Road
in autumn; a bear
cub lounges happily
in a tree.

Right:
Parson Branch Road
takes you deep into
a mature hardwood
forest.

● 4
BUNKER HILL QUIET WALKWAY

The path to your right offers a ridge-top walk through pine-oak forest—prime habitat for bear and wild hog.

The stream to your left is Parson Branch, which you can follow on down to road's end and Highway 129. From here the road levels

out, curves among laurel thickets through magnificent tall trees, and crisscrosses the maturing stream several times. Watch and listen to its growth as you go.

● 5
PARSON BRANCH CROSSING

Parson Branch gradually becomes a respectable little tumble of whitewater. This is a good place to stop again, absorb the sights and sounds and smells once more, tuck them into your psyche to take home with you. Places like this don't come along very often.

BUNKER HILL

This prominent peak is thought to have been given this name for no apparent reason except that it needed a name and someone suggested Bunker Hill, a patriotic one. It was not uncommon in the early days to name places after other famous places or people.

● 6
EXIT

Parson Branch Road ends here at U.S. 129. Turn right, and you meander through the mountains and along the scenic shore of Chilhowee Lake for about 10 miles to the west terminus of the Foothills Parkway. Straight ahead at that junction would take you on through Maryville and into Knoxville.

Turning left, Highway 129 winds southeasterly into North Carolina, through the Snowbird Mountains. Either way you turn, be extra careful. Motorcyclists use 129 for recreation, and some will be traveling at maniacal speeds.

Gatlinburg Bypass

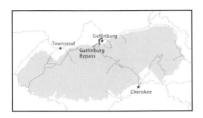

4 MILES
FROM U.S. 441 NORTH
OF GATLINBURG, TN TO
NEWFOUND GAP ROAD

The four-mile Gatlinburg bypass is also a park road, serving primarily as an access route. The bypass forks from U.S. 441 just north of the city, hugs the flank of Mt. Harrison as it skirts west of downtown Gatlinburg, and rejoins the park's over-mountain highway (Newfound Gap Road) north of Sugarlands Visitor Center. It provides not only a respite from the traffic, but excellent views and good photo opportunities from overlooks high above the busy resort town.

Gatlinburg's role, and that of other towns around the park's perimeter, is a valuable one. Because these towns provide essential visitor services—rooms, meals, shopping, and so on—the park can be managed exclusively for the preservation of its natural beauty. Imagine the impact if these millions of visitors had to be housed and fed within the park instead of outside it.

In the natural world it's called a symbiotic relationship: each nourishes the other in a vital interdependence.

Left:
Hoar frost on
Mt. Le Conte, viewed
from the Gatlinburg
Bypass

Right:
Gatlinburg, circa
1913. Taken from a
hill on Highway 321
looking toward
town

These lowlands along the Little Pigeon River were settled in the early 1800s by families drifting from many parts of the southern Appalachians. The community—called "White Oak Flats" at first—remained a remote settlement for decades, catering to regional vacationers who even then sought out the peace of the Great Smokies. Since the late 1930s, and especially after World War II, Gatlinburg's mushrooming growth has paralleled the increasing popularity of Great Smoky Mountains National Park, and it now attracts millions of visitors annually.

Left, from top: Gatlinburg, circa 1930, store and post office. Hitching pole and postman's horse are situated to the right of the store. The Mountain Mall near Ripley's Aquarium of the Smokies is located on this site today; Gatlinburg 2003; Gatlinburg, circa 1938. McDonald's restaurant on the Parkway is located on this site today.

Great Smoky Mountains Time Line

1540—Hernando De Soto explores the southern Appalachian Mountains and encounters the Cherokee, who had inhabited the region for centuries.

1775—Botanist William Bartram explores the southern Appalachians.

1795—Mingus and Hughes families clear homesteads in Oconaluftee River Valley.

1814—Caldwells establish first homestead in Cataloochee Valley.

CIRCA 1818-1821—First Euro-Americans settle in Cades Cove.

1819—Cherokee relinquish claim to the last of their lands in the Smoky Mountains.

1830—Population of Cades Cove is 271.

1838-39—Most of Cherokee tribe moved from Southeast to Oklahoma along the "Trail of Tears."

1839—Oconaluftee Turnpike between Oconaluftee and Indian Gap completed.

1850—Population of Cades Cove is 685.

1861-1865—American Civil War. Mountaineers are divided in their allegiances. Raiders on both sides frequently seize food, livestock, and other supplies from residents.

CIRCA 1870-75—John P. Cable Mill built in Cades Cove.

1882—Little Greenbrier School built.

1886—Mingus Mill built.

1900—Population of Cades Cove is 708.

1903-04—Lumber companies set up operations on Eagle and Hazel creeks.

1908—Elkmont logging camp constructed.

1910—Population of Cataloochee is 1,251.

1913—Horace Kephart's Our Southern Highlanders is published.

1934—Great Smoky Mountains National Park is established.

1939—Little River Lumber Company finishes cutting timber in the Tremont area.

Cherokee Orchard Road & Roaring Fork Motor Nature Trail

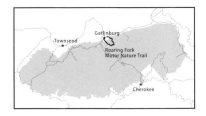

9 MILES
FROM DOWNTOWN GATLINBURG, TN TO END OF ROARING FORK MOTOR NATURE TRAIL

Cherokee Orchard and Roaring Fork Motor Nature Trail (closed in winter) are less than four miles from the modern bustle of Gatlinburg's main street. But they're many years away from those busy scenes, a plunge backward in human history and to intimate natural beauty. Many park visitors miss this rewarding diversion.

All the elements that make the Smokies special—the changing land, nature's variety and abundance, and the human legacy—combine to make this short outing a memorable one.

CHEROKEE ORCHARD ROAD

To reach Cherokee Orchard, drive up Historic Nature Trail-Airport Road (traffic light number 8 from Gatlinburg's main street), keep right past the turnoff for the big hotel atop the hill, and reenter the park on Cherokee Orchard Road. The Noah "Bud" Ogle Self-Guiding Nature Trail is just three miles from downtown, and the auto trail through Roaring Fork a half mile farther.

Left:
Roaring Fork

Right:
Entrance to Roaring Fork Motor Nature Trail

● 1

NOAH "BUD" OGLE PLACE

Many farms like this once dotted the hollows of the Smokies. A three-quarter-mile trail leads through the preserved heart of this one, and a self-guiding leaflet is available at the beginning of the loop.

The Ogles were one of the first Euro-American families to settle in the White Oak Flats (Gatlinburg) area in the early 1800s. "Bud" Ogle raised his large family here after the Civil War. His friends warned him that these 400 acres would be poor farming, but hard work proved them wrong.

Woods have reclaimed the cleared land, but the home, barn, and tub mill are as the Ogles left them. The preserved farmstead is a study in self-sufficiency and living in harmony with the natural world.

Left:
Noah "Bud" Ogle home.

Right, from top:
Noah "Bud" Ogle tub mill; Crested dwarf iris

The trail guide points out these old-fashioned ideas, which are taking on new importance today amid growing concerns about diminishing resources. We may not depend on tub mills to grind our grain nowadays, for instance, but good water is more critical—and more endangered—than it was when the Ogle place was a working farm.

CHEROKEE ORCHARD

Named for a commercial apple orchard and plant nursery once owned and operated by M. M. Whittle. It was established in the 1920s and named for the Cherokee Indian legacy of the area. With the coming of the park, the orchard, containing over 6,000 fruit trees, as well as other ornamental trees and shrubs, was abandoned. The word Cherokee, in their language, means cave people.

● 2
RAINBOW FALLS TRAIL

This hiking trail leads to one of the more popular Smokies' waterfalls. It's a 5.5-mile round trip, vigorous but not forbidding, made worthwhile by the 80-foot splendor of falls and cataracts as Le Conte Creek plunges in a shimmering spray down the face of a cliff.

Continuing four miles past the falls, the trail follows the ridge of Rocky Spur—with beautiful views across the lowlands down toward Gatlinburg—and on to the summit of Mt. Le Conte.

STOP

LARGE MOTOR HOMES, BUSES, OR TRAILERS PROHIBITED ON ROARING FORK MOTOR NATURE TRAIL!

● 3
ROARING FORK MOTOR NATURE TRAIL
(CLOSED IN WINTER)

This 5.5-mile, one-way drive is paved but narrow and winding, not for buses, trailers or large motor homes. It emerges on Low Gap Road, leading back to U.S. 321 at the northeast edge of Gatlinburg.

This is a good place to reflect not only on nature's wonders, but on the human spirit that lingers here. The road was cut as wagon passage about 1850, providing a way to market, to church and school, to visits with neighbors.

● 1*
CONTINUITY & CHANGE

The view from here is a long one. Hill follows hill until they all fade into the misty distance. Stop your car, turn off the engine, and be quiet. In a few moments life around you will return to normal after the wake of your intrusion passes.

The forest that tumbles down the mountains is a young one in the eyes of Nature. It is the product of many things that happened to it in the past. Soil, climate,

Note: Numbering sequence on posts restarts at #1 once Roaring Fork Motor Nature Trail is entered.

geology, lumbering and farming have made it what it is. Natural forces continue to work to produce change. As the new vegetation covers the scars made by man, one wave of growth sets the stage for another. Slowly the forest matures, and one kind of plant or animal replaces another in a natural cycle called succession. As succession runs its course, some elements of the present environment may not be here someday because they won't "fit" this place anymore.

Down the hill is a young cove hardwood forest. Chestnut oak, white oak, magnolia, maple, and tuliptree are a few members of that varied community. They prefer the lower and middle elevations, and the moisture of the coves and valleys.

Pines and a few oaks run out on the dry ridge to the right. Members of a more exclusive community, they comprise the pine-oak forest.

No matter how often you visit this scene, it will change very little. Succession takes slow, subtle steps and your lifetime is but a flashing moment in the long parade.

Left:
Rainbow Falls

Right, from top:
Red spotted Newt;
Roaring Fork

● 2

A Closer Look

Here the immediate impression is one of tall green walls—a hopelessly tangled mess. Slowly, this vegetative snarl will begin to sort itself out if you look closely. There's no telling what you'll see or hear if you remain quiet and still.

Some of the cove hardwoods are here: sweet birch with the small almond-shaped leaves; tuliptree with its fat, squarish ones; and the black locust whose tiny rows of leaflets oppose each other on long stems, giving a lacy effect against the sky. Huge hemlocks pierce their way through the canopy like bristly green bottle brushes.

Down lower, rhododendron accents the understory with its clusters of blossoms, or leathery evergreen leaves, depending on when you visit. To the left, wild grape vines drape a whole section, as if trying to hold everything together.

How did it all get here, and how does it survive? Two ingredients are necessary: abundant rainfall and a prolonged period without frost, each year. Given those for a start, the broadleaf forest and its associates will do quite well.

Its "associates?" Birds, fox, raccoon, opossum, bear, chipmunk, mice, and groundhog. And there are ants, reptiles, beetles and many things too small for you to see.

The hot bright sunlight of the parking lot accents the coolness of the shady woods nearby. Walk a few steps into the forest. Acorns crashing to the ground, buzzing flies or drumming grouse will soon tell you that you're not alone.

 3

HAZE

If you've been here before as a child, you might remember another view. Now, on a clear day, you may be able to see Sugarland and Cove mountains. But the view here is more likely to be shrouded by a whitish haze, different from the mist-like clouds for which the Smokies were named.

Increasingly, visitors no longer see distant mountain ridges anywhere in the park. A very small portion of the haze is natural in origin; but there are other, unnatural forces at work here. Views have been seriously degraded over the last 50 years by human-made pollution, most of which originates outside the park.

Up the hill to the right is a quiet place, furnished with a bench. Enjoy it—unless someone has beaten you to it.

● 4
CHESTNUT LOGS

For the next few hundred feet the roadside is littered with fallen chestnut trees. They were killed by blight in the early 1900s; yet many stumps still survive. New growth sprouts from the stumps, but eventually succumbs to the disease of the parent tree.

There are few mature American chestnut trees left in the park. Blight-resistant strains are being developed elsewhere, but it will be many years before the seedlings attain the 5-6 feet in diameter size of their ancestors.

● 5
GROTTO FALLS PARKING LOT

The Trillium Gap Trail begins here, and ends on top of Mt. Le Conte. The first 1.3 miles are through an old-growth forest of hemlock trees to Grotto Falls.

The walk to Grotto Falls is fairly easy, as the trail climbs only 520 feet along the way. The trail is shaded by large American beeches, silverbells, and maples.

After leaving Grotto Falls, the trail climbs steeply to Trillium Gap and on to the summit of Mt. Le Conte. This four-mile leg of the trail rises about 3,400 feet through more hemlock, and into red spruce and Fraser fir.

Left, from top:
Grotto Falls; Trillium Gap Trail passes behind the falls

Right:
Trail to Grotto Falls among the hemlocks

● 6
HEMLOCK TREES

You have just topped out and are heading down into the Roaring Fork watershed. With windows open the change and feel of the air are suddenly noticeable. It is cooler and you are surrounded by tall, straight evergreen hemlock trees. Old-timers called this place "the Spruce Flats." That was an unfortunate misnomer, because the trees here aren't spruce, and there isn't much flat ground.

The hemlock forest is one of several distinct tree communities in the Smokies. Hemlocks prefer a cooler, moister environment than some of the other trees. Under ideal conditions here, many hemlocks reach world record sizes of 5-6 feet in diameter.

Unfortunately the park's hemlocks are under attack from a tiny Asian insect called the hemlock woolly adelgid. This nearly microscopic bug has the potential to kill most of the region's hemlock trees. The National Park Service and several partner organizations are working on a number of methods to fight the invasion, including releasing predator beetles that feed solely on hemlock adelgids.

● 7
TULIPTREES

You may have noticed that the hemlocks gave way to tuliptrees rather abruptly. That's because the cornfields where the tuliptrees stand ended abruptly. They are the tall slim trees with the light gray bark.

The tuliptrees are a pioneer tree; they sprout up quickly where open land is abandoned. They will continue to thrive for a long time, but will be shaded out by the hemlock forest growing up through them now.

The tuliptrees reveal that this place was once cleared and farmed. This, the Clabo farm, was almost the "upperest" home. The old spring is nearby, and the first sounds of Roaring Fork reach you here. It will grow in size and start to roar as you follow the old road down the mountain.

Vehicle break-ins sometimes occur at trailheads. Lock your car and keep purses, cameras, portable stereos, and other valuables on your person or lock them in the trunk before you get to the trailhead.

BUILDING STYLES OF THE SMOKIES

HOMES

single pen

saddlebag

dog-trot

BARNS

two-pen drive
through

shotgun

four-pen
cantilever

● 8
OLD ROAD

The Roaring Fork community was settled about 170 years ago by people in search of new ground to farm. In the 1830s and '40s this was a frontier. The turn of this century found the mature little hamlet stabilized at about two dozen families. This was enough to support a few small tub mills, a store, a church and a school. The village was not a crossroads to anywhere. It was a dead end. Below lay Gatlinburg, a place unto itself. Above stood mountains whose names say something: Piney, Brushy, Rocky Spur, Scratch Britches.

The stream is a crooked crease in the lumpy skirts of Mt. Le Conte. Settlers followed it because it ran through the most nearly level land, in a place where there is no level land.

The road followed the stream. For the next half-mile you will travel on the old roadbed, which dates back to about 1850. Be thankful you're going down in a car, not up, on foot or in a wagon. The road was built with local labor, hard labor. During a "working," the men turned out with pick and shovel to level high spots, fill ruts and move rocks. Large boulders were blasted apart with powder or dynamite. Lacking that, they were

Defacing historic structures in the park is against the law and is punishable by fines of up to $5,000 and six months in prison.

heated with fire and cracked off with cold water. This was done year after year, but somehow the rocks never got fewer.

Transportation was slow in the mountains because road construction was difficult, and travel was hard on man, beast, and wagon. No one went anywhere unless they really needed to. There were few frivolous jaunts, for a round trip of several miles could consume the whole day.

● 9
WHERE DID THEY GO?

When the national park was established, the people living here had to leave. Over two-thirds of those that left the park were from Sevier County.

A few were given lifetime leases on their homes because they were too old or too sick to move. A few others were given special permits to allow them to stay on and farm. This didn't work out very well. The people couldn't farm in the ways they had learned in childhood. They couldn't cut firewood. They couldn't hunt and fish in the hills. In short, staying on was next to impossible, or not worth it, or both.

Right, from top: A photographer sets up his equipment to photograph Roaring Fork; a salamander forages through autumn leaves; the Alex Cole cabin

As this door closed, others opened. The tourist industry in Gatlinburg was just beginning to grow. There were fresh opportunities to build a new life just outside the park. Motels and restaurants, riding stables and craft shops were all new fields to plow and crops to harvest.

But not everyone stayed near home. Some followed the logging industry to the Great Northwest, since the logging boom here was over. The Motor City called, too. The dream of many young men was to "go to Dee-troit and work at the Ford place."

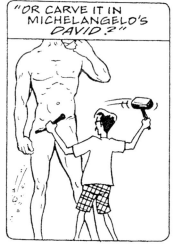

Most of these people can come home again, in a different sort of way. They can see the tall stands of tuliptrees where fields used to be, and the piles of rock where their fireplaces were. That elicits a certain sadness sometimes. Yet they know that these things will now not change anymore. They, their children, and their grandchildren can all return to this place that will always be.

● 10
HISTORIC PRESERVATION

The house across the stream is not on its original site. It was moved in from a regenerating wilderness area in order to assure its preservation. The corn crib and barn do belong here on this, the old Jim Bales place. The remaining buildings along this road are on original sites.

Moving historic structures is not a desirable practice for it destroys "site integrity"—the qualities of a building in relation to its surroundings. However, it is done when there are no, or poor, alternatives.

Why do we preserve such structures? What is their value?

Right, from top:
Roaring Fork Motor
Nature Trail;
Ephraim Bales place

When the European settlers entered this place, the environment was clearly in control. Settlers had to cope with the world on its terms—not theirs. In many ways these buildings help us to see how they managed to do that, to

shelter family and livestock, store food, protect tools and equipment, and earn a living. Without books, photographs, family papers or other prior knowledge, we can learn much of the people who lived here.

Should you deface or destroy any part of them, you are degrading a part of yourself. In the larger sense, you are a part of this community.

● 11

EPHRAIM BALES PLACE

"Hardscrabble" is one name for a place like this. Ephraim Bales was a farmer. He, his wife, Minerva, and their nine children lived crammed into this dog-trot cabin, which was a bit on the small side to begin with. But their situation was not at all unusual, and individual privacy was something these people knew little about. Life for the Bales family was as sparse and hard as the ground around them. "Eph" and "Nervie" owned 70 acres of rocks and cultivated 30 of them. The rest remained in timber for cooking, heating and construction use. As you wander through this farm, imagine trying to feed, clothe, and shelter your family on this mountainside.

The house was never larger than it is now, except for a missing back porch. The logs, though small, are skillfully worked. Puncheon (split log) floors were drafty and allowed an occasional snake to slide in, but did serve the purpose when there was no sawed lumber around. Small doors conserved heat and let one finish the house without adding logs just to make the doorway higher. The large cabin was the living area; the smaller one, the kitchen. Additional beds stood in the once-closed-in dog-trot. The only window is the small "granny hole," which looks out on the family pantry-the corn crib. As one who knew him put it, "old Eph kept his rifle hangin' right here over the window. If he heard the shutter squeak on the corn crib, he took his rifle down." In front of the hearth is the 'tater' hole. It was a simple matter to lift a puncheon, withdraw some potatoes and toss them into the ashes to bake. When people couldn't grow enough corn for year-round use, potatoes carried them through.

The corn crib stands beside the house. Small, almost fragile, it is typical of many outbuildings on Roaring Fork. Its size tells us something about life here. Building required trees and hard work, so no one built anything larger than necessary. Why build a large crib when a large corn crop was practically impossible?

Up the hill stands the barn, which housed a mule and a cow. It must have been a small mule, or else it couldn't have gotten through the stall door. The loft was floored, to hold fodder for the animals, which was fed to them from a sloping rack on the wall and the grain box in the corner. Corn was stored in the adjacent crib. The diagonal scar on the lower side of the barn and the braces inside the roof betray one of the Bales' fears—wind. Except for the house, all the buildings are relatively light, and all were braced against the gales.

Left, from top:
Ephraim Bales barn;
Bales corn crib;
Minerva Bales

Right:
Alfred Reagan house
painted in "all three
colors [of paint] that
Sears and Roebuck
had."

● 12
ALFRED REAGAN PLACE

Alfred Reagan, like Ephraim Bales, was a farmer. He had cattle and crops, fruit trees and timber; and Mrs. Reagan had her flowers. But he had other things too: well-developed manual skills and the business sense to do something with them. A jack-of-all trades, he practiced most of them close to where you stand. His carpentry tools left their mark all over Roaring Fork community. A death in the neighborhood usually sent Reagan to his shop to make the coffin—free of charge.

The rocky mountainside was hard on farm equipment and wagons, so he saw a chance to fill a local need, and to make a little extra money. A blacksmith shop soon appeared beside the creek, where he mended things that wore out at home or shook apart on the road. There wasn't enough custom work in that alone, so he found another source of income. After all, the family now included several children.

By about 1900 Roaring Fork was large enough to need a store. Reagan built one. It stood beside the road and snared much of the local traffic. Apparently preferring heavier work, he turned the store over to a son, whose job was to keep it stocked and open. Doing this meant wholesale buying trips to Knoxville, then several days away by wagon.

Either not content with his holdings, or still bursting with energy, Reagan capped his enterprises with a mill. Everyone needed bread, yet not everyone had the tools or know-how to build a mill. As was customary, he charged one gallon per bushel in toll for grinding, which he doubtless converted to cash in some way. Alfred Reagan learned one of the secrets of stability and success that many others did not—diversity. In his more active years he was even a lay preacher in the church that he helped build, on land that he donated.

By now you must have heard the splash of water on the tiny mill wheel. Dozens of "tub mills" stood ankle deep on spindly legs along mountain streams of low volume and high velocity. Their primitive turbines spun their way from ancient Europe and Asia to the hills of eastern America. Reagan's mill was a good one, so we're told. Its precise construction allowed it to run when others were shut down for lack of water. The flume, which carries water to the mill, was important to the folk who passed by. It was a good place to water your horse, clean a few squirrels after a hunt, or plunge your face on a hot day. Mrs. Reagan did her laundry in it, too.

The Reagans took a fine house and made it finer. It is a "saddlebag house," the two halves hanging from a central chimney. The form wasn't unique, but was not very common either. The hewing is clean, the corners tight, and the log ends cut flush with each other, as though the builder knew that some day it would be sheathed with fine boards. At some time, probably after the Reagan's fifth or sixth child, they raised the roof to create the attic bedrooms and added the kitchen wing at the rear. The "new house" deserved sawed board paneling and ceilings, slicked down with a hand plane. "All three colors [of paint] that Sears and Roebuck had" set the house off nicely against its mountain backdrop. Inside, the family sat, slept, and ate on furniture from Alfred Reagan's own hands.

Left:
Tub mill on Roaring Fork

Right, from top:
Water rolls easily over moss covered rocks in Roaring Fork; Wakerobin and Yellow trillium

● 13

WATER

Roaring Fork is a classic mountain stream in every way. It is clear, cold, ever-flowing, shady, fast and noisy. Listen. It will talk to you all day, but never say the same thing twice.

For all its rushing and dashing to get downhill, the stream does some things slowly and thoroughly. Find a rock with a pothole in it. Now find a spot where the water swirls in a little whirlpool. The scouring action of water and sand, day-after-day for maybe hundreds of years, is what made the hole. And it polished the slick rocks that litter the streambed.

During its cycle from sky to sea, water seldom displays itself so well as a sustainer of life and creator of beauty as it does here.

● 14

BOULDERS

The boulder fields throughout this landscape must have gained your attention by now. They were painfully obvious to the local farmers. We do not know if, when they picked up a rock and dropped it on a sled to be dragged away, they ever paused and pondered its origin. Probably not. Perhaps farmers cursed them as the thousandth one was hurled from the field, yet praised them as their cabin's chimney neared completion.

How did they get here? The climate during the last ice age was much colder than now. Great sheets of ice and glaciers a few hundred miles north made for long cold winters and short summers here in the Smokies.

These conditions caused rocks to split from high mountain peaks. With each freezing and thawing cycle, boulders would tumble down the mountains in roaring masses, or inch their way imperceptibly over centuries. Whichever their mode of arrival, they came to rest in ravines as here.

PLACE OF A THOUSAND DRIPS

Named for an 80-foot high rock bluff above Roaring Fork. Cliff Branch spreads out to produce countless small falls and cascades that eventually join Roaring Fork along a 55-foot wide area. The falls vary from a trickle to a torrent depending on recent rainfall.

● 15

WATERFALLS

Called "Place of a Thousand Drips," this waterfall is cutting away at bedrock. You are watching the formation of a side canyon, although you will never live to see the finished product. A place of beauty; it is also home to water-loving plants— mosses, liverworts, and ferns.

Like other waterfalls in the park, the air around this one is moist and cool, the coolness being caused by evaporation. Pause, and enjoy the feel of natural refrigeration.

Left:
Roaring Fork

Right:
Place of 1,000 Drips

● 16

BOUNDARY

Shortly you will break into the "real world," for most of us one of cars and houses, power lines and paved streets. Where you have been is natural, although through the irony of civilization, it has become uncommon. We hope that Roaring Fork will always remain a "place of being," a place to get lost for a few moments, while regathering human strength from its original sources.

Greenbrier

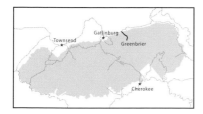

People who return to the Smokies time and again soon develop affection for their "special" places—usually quiet places, off the busier paths, a nook or cranny with its own distinct and enduring appeal. Greenbrier is one of those.

It's a short (five miles) country lane along the broad and burbling Little Pigeon River, six miles east on U.S. 321 from its intersection with U.S. 441 in Gatlinburg. The road's developed features include a small, cool picnic area three miles ahead in the woods at river's edge, a fairly challenging but immensely rewarding hiking trail to a magnificent waterfall, Ramsey Cascades, and Porters Creek Trail, one of the best spring wildflower walks in the country.

The greenbrier is a leather-tough but resilient little vine that clings to the rocky slopes with stubborn roots—a good metaphor for the hundreds of hardy souls whose homes were once where the park is now. Their cabins were scattered throughout the lowlands, but here and there—as in Greenbrier— several were clustered in small communities.

(Two of these were called "Greenbrier." To differentiate, this valley was Big Greenbrier: a settlement just north of what's now Metcalf Bottoms Picnic Area off Little River Road was Little Greenbrier.)

Though there were more pragmatic reasons as well, settlers were no doubt drawn to the Little Pigeon and its tributaries by something spiritual. The greenery—woods and shrubs and wildflowers—decorates the rocky slopes like a natural garden. The river is wide and handsome, the forested bottomland fertile and inviting.

*Left:
Little Pigeon River
along Greenbrier
Road*

*Right:
Upper Greenbrier
Road*

Notice how the water's force has sculpted river rock into smoothly curved, impressionistic shapes. There are many places to stop and linger, wade, or fish, with easy access all along the road.

Pavement ends in one mile at the ranger station, but gravel makes a good surface all the way to road's end in four miles.

At the bridge and through the woods, the trail to Ramsey Cascades begins 1.5 miles away. From there it's an eight-mile round-trip hike through a corridor of giant trees, along the roaring cascade, and beneath a sheer, thousand-foot cliff. The trail climbs about 2,400 feet in its four miles to the falls—easier coming down, but a challenging trip for those not accustomed to a bit of exercise. Few trails in the park, however, have as much to offer.

By going straight you will reach an impressive picnic shelter a half mile ahead—the site of many family reunions and special gatherings. A half-mile farther the road dead ends, and from there Porters Creek Trail ascends 3.6 miles through old-growth forest and blossoming glades. Even a one-mile stroll on this wide path will be rewarding.

GREENBRIER, ELEVATION 1,716'

Left, from top: Flowers bloom along a Smoky Mountain stream; Little Pigeon River along Greenbrier Road

Wildflower Blooming Schedule

JANUARY—Witch hazel's bright yellow flowers linger from the previous year.

FEBRUARY—Spicebush blooms. Trailing arbutus, daffodils, and periwinkle may bloom late in the month if the weather is mild.

MARCH—Mild weather will bring the following into bloom: sharp-lobed hepatica, bloodroot, spring-beauty, trout-lily, early meadowrue, Jack-in-the-pulpit.

APRIL—Spring woodland wildflowers usually reach their peak of bloom around mid-April. The park's annual wildflower pilgrimage is held during the last full week of the month. Visit www.springwildflowerpilgrimage.org or call (865) 436-7318 for more information. Species in bloom include: fringed phacelia, purple phacelia, white trillium, Dutchman's britches, squirrel corn, wild geranium, yellow trillium, fire pink, violets, cut-leaved toothwort, large-flowered bellwort, crested dwarf iris, wild ginger, wood anemone, little brown jugs, and yellow mandarin.

MAY—May-apple, painted trillium, foamflower, brook lettuce, bleeding heart, lady's slippers, showy orchis, blue cohosh, columbine, wake robin, blue phlox, purple phacelia, wood betony, meadow-parsnip, umbrella leaf.

JUNE—Galax, fly poison, speckled wood lily, goat's beard, wood sorrel, yellow star grass, sundrops, squawroot, mountain spiderwort, rattlesnake hawkweed, Indian pink, woodland bluets, false hellebore, Canada mayflower.

JULY—Indian pipe, downy rattlesnake-plantain, wood tickseed, Michaux's saxifrage, ramps, mountain mint, butterfly weed, Rugel's ragwort, small purple-fringed orchid, thyme-leaved bluets, heal-all.

AUGUST—Whorled wood aster, mountain bugbane, cardinal flower, Turk's cap lily, mountain St. John's wort, filmy angelica, monk's hood, crane-fly orchid, mountain krigia, starry campion, sweet Joe-Pye-weed.

SEPTEMBER—Pink turtlehead, New York ironweed, jewelweed, yellow-fringed orchid, black-eyed Susan, Canada goldenrod, skunk goldenrod, love-vine.

OCTOBER—White wood aster, bee balm, Maryland golden aster, wide-leaved sunflower, coneflower, heart-leaved aster, stoneroot, mountain gentian.

NOVEMBER—Nodding lady's tresses, tall rattlesnake root, and southern harebell linger in bloom until the first frost.

DECEMBER—Witch-hazel blooms.

SHARP-LOBED HEPATICA

WILD GERANIUM

BISHOP'S CAP

BLOODROOT

BLUE PHLOX

SQUIRREL CORN

CRESTED DWARF IRIS

FRINGED PHACELIA

BLUETS

Cataloochee

39 MILES
FROM CHEROKEE, NC TO
CATALOOCHEE VALLEY

Tucked into the remote southeastern corner of the Smokies is a well-concealed place of special beauty, discovered by a special few. To many of those who seek out "the lost cove of Cataloochee," it is the spiritual heart of the park.

Two roads lead to Catalooch', as it's familiarly known. One is a demanding 27-mile drive, mostly gravel, from Cosby around the eastern end of the park. The easier alternative is via Interstate 40 from the U.S. 276 exit at the southeast corner of the park. The 11-mile Cove Creek Road is partly paved as it winds up to the gap and into the cove. The two approaches are described separately here.

While it seems far off the park's well-beaten path, Cataloochee was the scene of surprising human busyness not long ago, a bustling community of more than 1,200 people— biggest settlement in the Smokies, and the fount of many legends. Its roads, now silent, were a major thoroughfare for early travelers through the

*Right, from top:
Cataloochee Valley;
sumac*

mountains, used by animals, Indians, and European settlers long before automobiles and interstate highways were even imagined.

Around the turn of the 20th century nearly 200 buildings were scattered around the picturesque cove. Only a handful now remain, poignant memorials to a lively past.

But the natural beauty that greeted

pioneers 150 years ago is unchanged: a long, narrow valley surrounded by the high Smokies, the timeless turbulence of Rough Fork and Pretty Hollow Creek watering the cove's woods and pastures. Deer and elk now graze untroubled where cattle once roamed, and Wild Turkeys have reclaimed the fertile fields from their domesticated cousins.

CATALOOCHEE VALLEY, ELEVATION 2,680'

Humans are still drawn to Cataloochee, as they have been since the unknown ancestors of the Cherokee followed bison that gathered here to graze. Today people come to visit, to camp, to view wildlife and discover this isolated splendor for themselves. Others, whose family roots run deep, gather here each summer for a thoughtful reunion.

Its remoteness makes the discovery almost startling, and quite personal—a sinuous drive through the backcountry, and suddenly you top the gap to descend into a long, narrow bowl of flatland surrounded by green peaks and drained by pristine waters, here and there the home, farm, church, or school of humans who lived here a century before you came. It's a discovery well worth making. Here's how to find it for yourself:

FROM COSBY

The more challenging route into Cataloochee begins at the Cosby post office 18 miles east of Gatlinburg. There (where U.S. 321 meets U.S. 321/State 32 and makes its "T") turn right and check your odometer. No mileposts are used on this route, so references are given to the distance you've traveled.

At 1.2 miles is the turnoff to Cosby Campground, Picnic Area, and Self-guiding Nature Trail—a spot worth visiting even if you aren't staying overnight. And a good alternative campground, by the way, when the more popular park sites are full.

The well-developed campground and picnic areas are two miles up the drive along Cosby Creek. Highlights of the camp are its trails, including the self-guiding nature trail, which provides a leaflet to help heighten your sensory awareness of the natural world. Other trails, a bit longer, lead to scenic overlooks, the Appalachian Trail, and waterfalls. Ask at the camp office for directions.

Back on the main road (State 32) you may follow the pavement 10 more miles to the Tennessee-North Carolina state line, curving along the park boundary all the way.

Pavement ends at the state line, crossing the Appalachian Trail at Davenport Gap, and the road descends into Mt. Sterling

community on Big Creek. One mile up the right-hand road is the Big Creek Ranger station; the left-hand road leads two miles to I-40. For Cataloochee, go straight ahead, up the hill.

(Do not take trailers or large motor homes beyond this point. Use the other route via I-40 instead.)

Keep right at the fork about a mile past Mt. Sterling Community, and follow the curvy mountain road 14 miles further to the pavement in Cataloochee. It remains a narrow road, with pullouts provided in case you meet someone coming from the other direction. A superfluous "15 mph" speed limit sign advises that this is not a route for those in a hurry.

Left, from top: Cataloochee Valley is a good place to view deer, elk, and other wildlife; visitors enjoy Cataloochee on horseback

Right: Afternoon light streams down on Cataloochee

The park boundary is 5.5 miles from the state line, almost 17 miles from your starting point in Cosby, and the road improves somewhat. Three miles further you cross Mt. Sterling Gap (elevation 3,894 feet); from here a hiking trail climbs 2.7 strenuous miles to a lookout tower atop Mt. Sterling, 2,000 feet higher than the gap.

Mt. Sterling Gap is a point of historic interest. Herds of buffalo probably created the first trail through the gap, followed by pre-historic Indians on their way to what is now Waynesville, NC. Civil War Colonel George W. Kirk led 600 federal troops through Mt. Sterling Gap in April, 1865 to attack sites in western North Carolina.

About 2.5 miles past the gap a primitive road (closed by a gate) forks right. This is the "main street" of Little Cataloochee, smaller suburb of Big Cataloochee just over the ridge. The old road passes the Hannah Cabin and Little Cataloochee Baptist Church and dead-ends in about two miles. You're welcome to visit this smaller scenic cove, but it's foot traffic only.

As you head on toward Cataloochee after many up-and-down curves, you may

MARK HANNAH

Mark Hannah was one of the first park rangers in Great Smoky Mountains National Park. Born in 1906 in Little Cataloochee, his family's roots in the area stretched back to the 1820's when his great-grandparents began farming within the valley.

When the national park was formed in the 1930s, forcing Cataloochee residents to leave their homes, Hannah served as an important link between the displaced families and the government, smoothing the transition from private land to national park.

Hannah fought to preserve the history and heritage of the people of the Great Smokies. He was instrumental in the preservation of the buildings you see today in Cataloochee.

He also collected first hand accounts of the history of the mountain people, which are preserved in the park's archives. You can hear recorded stories of these early settlers in the visitor center at the Palmer House.

Mark retired from the Park service in 1971. He is remembered as a man who spent his life working to preserve Cataloochee and its memories.

appreciate the lament of Francis Asbury, a dedicated Methodist circuit-riding missionary back in the winter of 1810. He recorded his trip through here— perhaps his 60th sojourn through this rugged country— this way in his journal:

"I rode, I walked, I sweat, I trembled, and my old knees failed. Here are gullies, and rocks, and precipices... but O, the mountains! Height after height."

After getting lost, losing his footing in the rushing creeks, and struggling through Cataloochee's trackless thickets, his party finally emerged late at night, cold and hungry.

"What an awful day," he wrote, *"Last night I was strongly afflicted with pain."*

(Today's auto adventure seems tame by comparison.)

Your own respite is at hand. Seven miles past Mt. Sterling Gap the road makes a "T"–turn right. Less than a mile ahead the road flattens into the cove, and another mile brings you to pavement and the comfort of Cataloochee.

FROM I-40

The easier route is also the more scenic. I-40 through the Pigeon River gorge is one of America's prettiest Interstate drives and a joy in itself. From its interchange with U.S. 276 (Exit 20), drive two-tenths of a mile and turn right onto Cove Creek Road. It's a beautiful drive up the valley toward the mountains. The pavement ends after four miles, and there is gravel for approximately three miles before the pavement resumes. The graveled segment is narrow, has sharp curves, and may be rough at times.

Left:
Jim and Melissa Hannah lived in a log house built by Jim's father in 1864.

Right, from top: Cataloochee Creek; bridge across Cataloochee Creek; Little Cataloochee Baptist Church— when a member of the Little Cataloochee community died, the church bell would be rung for several minutes to attract attention. Then, after a brief pause, the bell would toll the age of the deceased.

Cove Creek Gap is the park boundary; two miles farther is an excellent place to pause, with fine views especially from the walk-up observation point on the knoll. The ridge south of you is the Cataloochee Divide, marking the park's southeastern boundary, and the peak to the east is Hazel Top.

As you head down the scenic descent into the cove you're treated with outstanding views northward across the Cataloochee Valley—Whiteoak Mountain to the right, Canadian Top (honoring a lumberjack who moved here from the North Woods), Noland Mountain, Cataloochee, and Balsam High Top towering in the distance.

CATALOOCHEE VALLEY

■ WILL MESSER BARN

Built by Will Messer about 1900, this barn stood on his farm in Little Cataloochee. It was moved here and restored in 1977 to better preserve this example of Messer's craftsmanship. Except for the ornate roof design, it is typical of many such outbuildings that once clung to the hillsides of Big and Little Cataloochee.

Left, from top: Farming and logging operations left the land in Cataloochee much more open than it is today; Will Messer barn; Palmer Chapel. Circuit riding ministers conducted church services once a month, but Sunday school was held every week.

■ PALMER CHAPEL

Religion entered Cataloochee with the Indians, but the white settlers preferred their own brand. Land for this Methodist Church was deeded by Mary Ann Palmer in 1898, and the building went

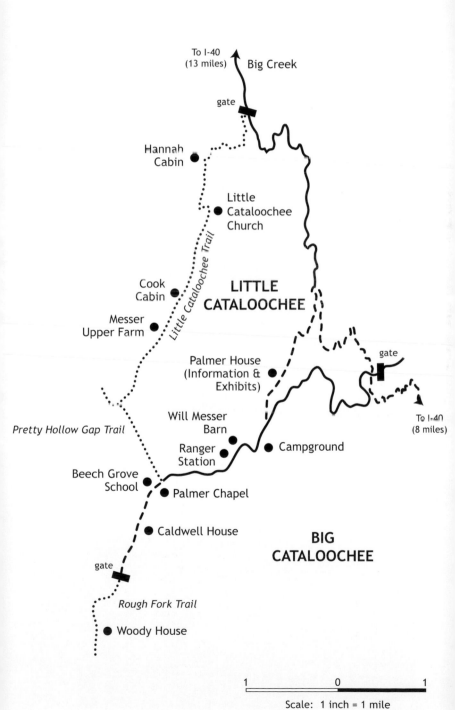

To I-40
(13 miles)
Big Creek

gate

Hannah
Cabin

Little
Cataloochee
Church

Cook
Cabin

Little Cataloochee Trail

Messer
Upper Farm

**LITTLE
CATALOOCHEE**

Palmer House
(Information &
Exhibits)

gate

To I-40
(8 miles)

Will Messer
Barn

Pretty Hollow Gap Trail

Ranger
Station

Campground

Beech Grove
School

Palmer Chapel

Caldwell House

**BIG
CATALOOCHEE**

gate

Rough Fork Trail

Woody House

——— Paved Road

- - - Gravel Road

········ Trail

1   0   1

Scale: 1 inch = 1 mile

up in the same year. Preachers were supplied by the Western North Carolina Conference of the Methodist Episcopal Church. Most of them were circuit riders who visited about one Sunday each month. Services consisted of prayers, singing, and sermons. Revivals held each fall rekindled the spirits of the faithful and brought in new members.

Even today a reunion is held each year at the church. Friends and families return to clean the cemeteries, attend services, and have dinner on the grounds.

■ BEECH GROVE SCHOOL

As the wilderness gave way to settlement, Cataloocheans provided schooling for their children. Three school districts built and operated schools in the valley: Big Cataloochee, Little Cataloochee, and Caldwell Fork. Big Cataloochee's Beech Grove School is the only one of the three that remains. It was built in 1901 to replace an older log building.

Schooling followed the laws and curriculum prescribed by the state. By the 1920s the term varied, but normally it ran from November through January. If sufficient local funds could be collected (subscriptions), it continued through February and March.

School began at 8 a.m. and let out at 4 p.m., with two recesses and a lunch hour. Children usually ate in family groups, the older ones being in charge of the little ones. The lunch bucket was usually jammed with sweet potatoes, cornbread, beans, applesauce, biscuits, ham, and a jar of milk.

Left:
The students of Beech Grove school in 1908. School attendance was usually good, since Cataloocheans respected education and supported the teachers' efforts.

Right, from top: Caldwell House; Hiram Caldwell moved his family from this log cabin into the large frame house now preserved by the park. Built in the 1840s, this cabin was thought to be the oldest log home still standing in Cataloochee when the park was established.

Subject matter included reading, writing, spelling, arithmetic, geography, and grammar. Friday was parents' day. They came in the afternoon to see what the children had accomplished that week. Spelling bees, recitations, and singing were both a test and an outlet for the pupils' pride.

School days ended in Cataloochee soon after the park was established. Relocation of families to communities outside left the desks empty, the blackboard dusty, and the building a lot quieter than it used to be.

■ CALDWELL HOUSE

Hiram Caldwell and his family lived for a long time in the old Levi Caldwell log house here on Rough Fork. In 1903, he decided it was time for a new home. Typical of houses to come, his new place (completed in 1906) was a modern framed structure with weatherboarding, as well as interior paneling "imported" from Waynesville, NC, about 25 miles away. The shingled gables reflected the nationally popular Eastlake style of the day. Hiram's large home was comfortable, and its beauty enhanced by handmade furniture from Cosby, Tennessee.

Old traditions persisted in the new home. The warping and quilting frames, spinning wheel and loom stood ready upstairs. The family's sheep yielded wool that padded quilts, was woven into cloth, and was sold or traded for goods on the open market. While the women did their household chores, the men and boys farmed and managed livestock on the high mountain pastures.

By the 20th century, Cataloochee was changing, and that change was reflected in the Caldwell home. Business affairs, tourists, and renters added variety and interest to the daily routine of family life.

Defacing historic structures in the park is against the law and is punishable by fines of up to $5,000 and six months in prison.

■ WOODY HOUSE

This home is accessible via an easy one-mile walk along Rough Fork Trail which begins at the end of Cataloochee Road.

Jonathan Woody entered Cataloochee before the Civil War, moved out for a while, and returned around 1866. A widower in his early 40s, he married Levi Caldwell's widow, Mary Ann, and moved into her cabin with his five youngest children. Nine of Mary Ann's 12 children were still living at home, creating one rather large family.

When Jonathan died in 1894, his son Steve Woody became head of the household. Starting with a one-room log cabin, Steve enlarged the home between 1901-1910 with framed additions, including several bedrooms, porches, and a kitchen.

His eight children slept upstairs in the "old soldiers' room" and awoke each morning to the sound of their mother grinding coffee. The usual farm and household work was relieved by supplemental tasks: gathering chestnuts, robbing beehives, hunting, and trapping.

Like many Cataloochee families, the Woodys took advantage of tourism that spilled into the lovely valley. They stocked the streams on their property with rainbow trout, and charged fishermen for the privilege of taking them. Sightseers and boarders slept in the house and barn, and ate in the home. The extra income was welcome. The Woodys, like their neighbors, saw the times changing and changed with them. The house is a good example of that: a progressive 20th-century structure with a log cabin heart.

■ PALMER HOUSE

In the 1840s George Palmer was living some miles away in Buncombe County. Succumbing to poor judgment and bad luck, he partook of a game of chance and lost a considerable sum of money. Ashamed to face his friends and relatives, poor George packed his family and belongings on the wagon and went in search of a new home. A few days later (the year was 1848) the Palmer family landed in Cataloochee, then sparsely populated and seemingly a good place to start anew. Apparently, the lesson stuck, because George, his wife and their descendants became one of the most prosperous families in Cataloochee. George died in 1859, the victim of a heart attack while cutting a fallen tree out of the road.

George Lafayette Palmer (Uncle Fate, in later years) was 23, single, and living at home when his father died, but he eventually started a family. His brother Jesse was already married and living on his own property. By 1870 the brothers had accumulated considerable wealth through hard work and good management. The census of that year reveals a large acreage, significant farm production, and a net worth of $800-$1,000 each. Some of their market crops included corn, wheat, oats, rye, apples, honey, molasses, butter, eggs, pigs, sheep, cattle, tobacco, potatoes, and cordwood. Both were informal bankers, lending money at interest and securing it with livestock and land. Jesse and Uncle Fate were also public-spirited, each serving as land assessor, justice of the peace, election judge, road trustee, and church official.

Left:
Steve Woody Place

Right, from top:
George Lafayette
"Uncle Fate" Palmer
and his wife Nancy
Jane Colwell Palmer;
the Jesse Palmer
home now houses
exhibits

The brothers built similar houses around 1860; this one belonged to Uncle Fate. It is a classic "dog-trot" house—two log structures side by side, an open area between, and covered with a common roof. It was nice enough as a double log house, with cooking/eating space on one side and living/sleeping space on the other. About 1901-05, Uncle Fate and his grown son Jarvis weather boarded the outside and ceiled the inside with hand-planed paneling. When Uncle Fate died in 1910, Jarvis inherited the place. Outbuildings included the large barn, blacksmith shop, springhouse, and now-absent can house and smokehouse.

Jarvis was an early entrepreneur in the tourism business. Members of his family owned land and controlled the fishing rights along almost three miles of Cataloochee Creek. They stocked the stream and charged 50¢ per day to fish. An angler who paid the daily fee was given a large metal "Palmer

Button" to indicate the fee had been paid. The button was displayed prominently on the fisherman's hat. Harley Palmer patrolled the creek to make sure visitors were in compliance.

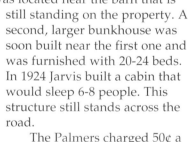

The Palmers allowed people to camp on their land while fishing. Around 1917 Jarvis built a two-room bunkhouse that would sleep 8-10 people. The bunkhouse was located near the barn that is

still standing on the property. A second, larger bunkhouse was soon built near the first one and was furnished with 20-24 beds. In 1924 Jarvis built a cabin that would sleep 6-8 people. This structure still stands across the road.

The Palmers charged 50¢ a day to stay in one of the bunkhouses and an additional 50¢ per day for meals served at the Palmer house.

To accommodate diners, Jarvis added a two-room kitchen and dining wing on to the south end of the house in about 1924. Those two rooms now house the park's visitor information display and audio visual program. Jarvis's wife Velma and his sister Maria handled the cooking and housekeeping.

When the park was established, Jarvis's family moved out and a ranger moved into their home.

■ A Gathering Place

The post office and general store served as a daily gathering place for Cataloochee residents and were the centers of community life in the valley. Here residents could mail a letter or exchange gossip.

Several post offices operated in the valley during the early 1900s. The Nellie Post Office, named after a daughter of "Turkey" George Palmer, operated out of one side of a general store near Palmer Chapel. The Ola Post Office in Little Cataloochee was named after the daughter of Will Messer, and also operated out of a general store.

A third post office was located in the Palmer house. As you face the Palmer house today, the room to the left of the porch was the Cataloochee Post Office from the early 1900s until the time the family moved away from the park. Aunt Maria Love Palmer acted as postmistress.

Left, from top: Fisherman's bunkhouse. Cataloocheans took advantage of the developing tourist industry by stocking streams with rainbow trout and building cabins to lodge visiting anglers; footbridge in Cataloochee

Right, from top: "Turkey" George Palmer; Nellie Post Office

■ A Developing Tourism Industry

Beginning in the early 1900s, residents of Cataloochee saw an opportunity to earn some extra cash from the growing number of people who came to the valley for recreation.

In addition to the Palmers and the Woodys, other families developed tourist operations in the valley as sport fishing became a local industry. Will Hall created a small camp for fishermen near the present-day group camping area in the valley. Using mules and a drag he had scooped out a 3-acre pond beside Cataloochee Creek. He and his wife provided lodging in their home and in two cabins he built. If fishermen had bad luck in the creek, Hall charged 50 cents a piece for trout from his pond.

Elk Reintroduction

In the spring of 2001, the National Park Service released 25 elk into the wilds of the Great Smoky Mountains. It's the first time elk have roamed the Smokies in at least 150 years. Elk once ranged throughout much of the eastern United States, but were eliminated from the region by over-hunting and loss of habitat.

Since the release, many of the elk have remained in the vicinity of Cataloochee Valley. They are sometimes sighted in the open fields during mornings and evenings.

The release was part of a larger program to experimentally reintroduce elk to Great Smoky Mountains National Park. The park service released another two dozen elk in 2002.

Do not approach wildlife too closely. If your presence causes an animal to change its direction of travel, stop feeding, or change its behavior in any other way,

YOU ARE TOO CLOSE! Carry binoculars, or if you're a photographer, a long telephoto lens.

This experimental reintroduction is part of the park service mission to preserve native plants and animals on park lands. If a native species has been eliminated from a park, the agency may choose to reintroduce it. River otters and Peregrine Falcons have been successfully reintroduced to the Smokies.

■ CREATION OF THE NATIONAL PARK

At the height of their prosperity, Cataloochee communities evaporated. In 1928 rumors that the government would buy all their land to establish Great Smoky Mountains National Park amazed residents. By 1938 all but a few families had moved out to make way for the park.

Only fragments remain today of the once-thriving community of Cataloochee—bits and pieces that serve to remind us of what life

Right:
Morning mist hugs
the fields in
Cataloochee Valley

here was like. This was the biggest settlement in the Smokies; at the beginning of the 20th century nearly 200 buildings were scattered around the picturesque cove. Only a handful are left, poignant memorials to a vibrant past.

The forest has now reclaimed much of Cataloochee's farmlands and orchards. From wilderness, to civilization, to wilderness in little more than one long lifetime is unusual to us. To the deer browsing by the ruins of a stone chimney, things are perfectly normal. It's just another pile of rock and fallen timber.

Heintooga Ridge & Balsam Mountain Roads

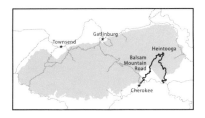

9 Miles
from the Blue Ridge
Parkway to Heintooga
Picnic Area

13 Miles
from Balsam
Mountain Road to Big
Cove Road

– Closed in Winter –

This is a loop tour—or a half-loop, if you prefer—beginning on the Blue Ridge Parkway a mile south of Oconaluftee Visitor Center. It climbs Balsam Mountain, with fine views along a mountain ridge, to a park campground and picnic area.

You could return by the same route. But to add another dimension, follow the one-way Balsam Mountain road along the ridge to Round Bottom and descend back into Cherokee by way of scenic Big Cove Road along Raven Fork. It's 20 miles to Heintooga Picnic Area from Cherokee; the unpaved Balsam Mountain-Round Bottom section covers 13 miles; then 12 more miles along the paved Big Cove Road returns you to the starting point.

The tour provides rich variety: lowland to high ridge, different terrain, and a range of perspectives from sweeping vista to hug-the-mountain intimacy. The paved portion is, of course, easy driving. The optional Balsam Mountain Road return (closed in winter) is narrow and winding as it follows the ridges, not suitable for trailers or large motor homes. For cars, it's primitive but no problem: the road is maintained and patrolled, and it's one-way with places to stop and enjoy its pleasures.

BLUE RIDGE PARKWAY
(FREQUENTLY CLOSED IN WINTER)

This famous scenic highway continues from this point along the mountain ridge all the way to Shenandoah National Park in Virginia, 469 miles away. One of America's great roads, it's beautiful at every mile and understandably attracts more than 20 million

visitors each year. A guidebook to the Blue Ridge Parkway, with details on its highlights, is available at the Oconaluftee Visitor Center.

In its 11 miles between here and the Wolf Laurel Gap turnoff, you'll climb to a mile-high elevation, pass through several rugged tunnels, and enjoy a number of overlooks with views in all directions. Ascent is steady, but it's an easy climb.

Notice the change in vegetation as you ascend. At higher elevations spring lags behind the valleys by two or three weeks. If you missed the flame azalea down lower, just drive up the mountain. In fall, the process is reversed.

Well-marked parkway points of interest won't be detailed here, but stop at the overlooks and learn from the displays. Note especially those at Thomas Divide viewpoint, about five miles ahead; the Big Witch (named for a famous Cherokee eagle hunter) two miles farther; and the descriptive road sign at the Qualla Reservation boundary, two miles more.

BLACK CAMP GAP

So named because a forest fire once partially burned a rustic structure in this camp that was often used by hunters as well as farmers ranging cattle in this area. Thereafter, campers often got black soot on themselves when they stayed in the partially charred structure.

HEINTOOGA RIDGE ROAD
(CLOSED IN WINTER)

After you turn here, the picnic area is nine miles farther. For three miles you're on a spur of the parkway—Heintooga Ridge Road—before re-entering Great Smoky Mountains National Park.

One and one-half miles after your turn is the Mile-High Overlook (actually 30 feet shy of a mile, but close enough). Weather permitting, this overlook provides a sweeping vista of the heart of the Smokies. A parkway interpretive marker tells more about the park's creation. Across the road, another overlook offers a fine view of lovely Maggie Valley to the east. Since you're riding the crest of the ridge, views will appear on either side of the road.

● 1
BLACK CAMP GAP

At this point you re-enter Great Smoky Mountains National Park. Picnic tables are available at the parking area, and a short path leads to a memorial erected by Masonic orders from around the country. The cairn, built when the park was created, incorporates stones collected from many parts of the world, and honors the public benevolence of the fraternal order.

Left, from top:
A view from Heintooga Ridge Road; Turk's cap lily

Right:
Heintooga Ridge Road meanders past a wall of cut rock

● 2
MOUNTAIN-MAKING

Here's a fine view of the Smokies, and—in rock cuts across the road and again a little farther along—visible evidence of continuing creation at work. Rocks loosened by rains fall, as weather continues trying to level the land. See how rock strata, originally layered horizontally more than 500 million years ago, have been lifted almost vertically by the enormous force of plate movements. Thick veins of quartz glisten white among the layers. They were born in volcanoes millions of years before the mountains, intruded into the sediment filling the Appalachian trough,

lifted mile-high by the buckling that made the mountains, and now stand exposed to share their ancient story.

● 3
Polls Gap

The weather gate just ahead is closed by rangers during winter. It's also a gateway into the Canadian-zone high country, where the scene changes dramatically. Almost suddenly spruce and fir dominate, mixed with Catawba rhododendron. The evergreens are found here only at higher elevations; they were isolated by the Ice Age and thrive in this cool, moist air. Although the ice cap did not reach this far south, the ice floors "pushed" northern

Balsam Mountain Campground, Elevation 5,310'

Polls Gap

Allegedly, Polly Moody's husband took their cows through this gap on the way to summer pasture. One year, he also took her favorite milk cow, which was pregnant at the time. As a result of the long and steep climb, the milk cow gave birth to her calf prematurely and both the cow and calf died. Polly threw such a tantrum over this loss that her neighbors named this gap Poll (short for Polly) in her honor.

HEINTOOGA

The word Heintooga is a corruption of the Cherokee I-yen-too-ga, meaning hiding place or refuge, or more literally, a dwelling in the wilderness or an inhabitant of the wilderness. Visible from the Heintooga Overlook is a vast wilderness, some of which was the last refuge of the Cherokees trying to avoid being expelled from their homeland in the 1830s along the infamous Trail of Tears.

vegetation southward. This area became a refuge for a number of northern species.

From Polls Gap, the Rough Fork Trail meanders eastward down to Cataloochee and Hemphill Bald Trail hugs the high country on its course along the Cataloochee Divide.

Left, from top:
Balsam Mountain
Campground at the
end of the season;
red spruce tree in
winter

● 4
BALSAM MOUNTAIN CAMPGROUND

At 5,310 feet, this is the highest of all the park's developed campgrounds. It's especially appealing in midsummer, with its mild days and delightfully cool nights. Here too is an adventure into the forests of the high country. The self-guiding nature trail—three-quarters of a mile long and easy walking—is an excursion into the different world of "alpine" woods, and a leaflet available at the trailhead will alert you to its wonders.

Right:
View from
Heintooga Overlook

● 5
HEINTOOGA OVERLOOK

The parking area here at the end of the paved road is gateway to rewarding discoveries. Enjoy a picnic 5,535 feet in the sky. Take a short walk to the "jump-off" view from Heintooga Overlook.

From the overlook, the trail continues back along Flat Creek through the majestic peace of a high-elevation northern hardwood and spruce-fir forest. The three-mile trail emerges back on the Balsam Mountain Road, three miles below the campground.

The end of the pavement is also the beginning of adventure; it awaits just beyond the parking area, through the gate and into the woods.

● 6

Balsam Mountain Road (Closed in Winter)

The Balsam Mountain Road is an easy route to adventure that combines the best of many worlds—intimate backcountry exploration, splendid mountain vistas, mile-high country, and river-bottom lowland. It's closed in winter, but is worth return visits other times for the beauty of spring all through summer, or the golden glory of fall.

Your first glimpse through the gate at Heintooga Overlook might make you wonder how "primitive" the one-lane, one-way drive might be. Don't fret. It's an easy drive, well tended, a bit "jostly" in spots perhaps but no problem for any vehicle smaller than a bus or oversized camper. Good ground clearance, no serious switchbacks or steep grades, no low overhang, adequately wide. Plunge ahead.

This one-way portion travels 13 miles along the ridge through splendid woods. Five more miles of good graveled road, then a scenic nine-mile paved highway along Raven Fork returns you to Cherokee. Total driving time from Heintooga back to U.S. 441 is about an hour. Give yourself longer for leisure, however.

Have your tree book and wildflower guide handy. This is a botanical showcase, abundant and varied from the 5,535-foot altitude at the start to about 2,000 feet in elevation along Raven Fork approaching Cherokee.

● 7

Northern Hardwoods Forest

Roadside flowers will probably get your attention immediately, along with the thick understory among the dappled shade of tall trees. Deciduous trees, notably the

Left:
The forest along Heintooga Ridge Road in a lonely fog

Right:
A wild hog and the damage wild hogs do in rooting the ground looking for food

American beech and yellow birch, dominate the forest community along the route. These "beech gaps," crowding out the evergreens, are something of a mystery even to botanists: what accounts for their dominance of certain areas?

Yellow birch is strikingly abundant here. Notice how its mottled bark peels away in papery wisps. These curls are said to be good in emergencies for starting fires.

A twig from the yellow birch, with the bark peeled back, releases a delightful wintergreen aroma and taste. They make dandy breath fresheners, and before nylon bristles came along were used as natural toothbrushes. As the trees mature the bark becomes

brown and deeply furrowed; you may spot some older birches along the route if you're alert. They're one of the taller deciduous trees, reaching more than 100 feet high and nearly five feet thick.

● 8

WILD HOG EXCLOSURE

Pens like these are a strange sight in the wild. But they're here because of an extraordinary problem. As the small sign tells you, this is an exclosure, one of several scattered throughout the park. They were placed in selected study areas to keep wild hogs out, to protect representative forest communities from their destructive rooting.

The exclosures give scientists a chance to study contrasts between areas foraged by hogs and those protected from them. By comparing areas, rangers can get an accurate picture of the type and extent of damage done by the pests.

The studies should help in understanding

hog impacts and eventually bring about a solution to a troublesome problem—the invasion of wild hogs. These animals aren't native, but unwelcome interlopers that escaped from nearby game lands over 90 years ago and began a

relentless march through the Smokies, unchecked by natural enemies, creating havoc with the delicate environment as their range expanded.

Today wild hogs forage across most of the park, rooting through the earth, eating plants, roots, bulbs, insects, and small animals—including rarities that should be protected. The hogs are tough, smart, and highly adaptable, so far resisting most control measures.

To check their expansion, reverse it, and ultimately remove the hogs from the park is a dilemma. Experts know it must be done, but in a way that does not harm other forms of life—those native species that belong here.

Visitors rarely catch a glimpse of the invaders, since they're highly elusive and mostly nocturnal. You may run across their feeding ground however—a large area devoid of plants, the earth plowed as if it had been turned by a garden tiller.

● 9

SMOKIES' CREST VIEWPOINT

On a clear day the views from here are across nearby ridges all the way to the heart of the Smokies nearly 15 miles away— Clingmans Dome, Newfound Gap, Mt. Kephart, Charlies Bunion, the Sawteeth.

It seems hard to believe that these lush woods you now drive through were heavily logged not many decades back. The graveled road you're traveling, in fact, follows an old, narrow-gauge railroad bed along the ridge called Balsam Mountain, winding with its contours and down the mountain through Round Bottom to the flatlands below.

Millions of board feet of virgin timber followed the route you now take, on their way to the sawmills and into the homes and buildings of a growing nation. But the tenacious land brings forth new life, and this abundant second-growth forest is the result. Here and there along the route you may spot some magnificent specimens that escaped the saw. They're testimony to the grandeur that once cloaked the Smokies.

● 10

DUTCHMAN'S PIPE

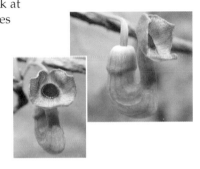

Take a look at those ropy vines draping some trees here. Large heart-shaped leaves distinguish the Dutchman's pipe, a treat any time but especially in late April to early June (depending on the altitude) when its unusual brown-and-yellow flower blooms. The blossom is curved into an S-shape with a bowl at one end, resembling the pipe that gives the vine its name. This is the upper limit of its range. It'll be a roadside decoration from here on down.

Left, from top: A hiking trail off of Heintooga; fly poison

Right, from top: Dutchman's pipe; view of the Smokies from Heintooga

In the midst of grandeur and sweeping vistas, don't miss the thousand little things like this that make the forest such a special place. The tiniest of flowers, the humblest plant, bird, beetle or salamander— all have a vital place, and cooperate to create a wonder.

Stay alert. You may see a bear, or hear the drumming of the Ruffed Grouse. You'll almost surely meet the Dark-eyed Junco, distinctive for his slaty color and white outer tail feathers. This is called the "snowbird," since its appearance at lower elevations marks the beginning of cold weather. (Some juncos that nest in the Smokies do not migrate from northern to southern horizons in winter; they accomplish the same purpose by a much easier trip down the mountain.)

● 11
HEATH BALD

There's no pullout here, but pause for a good view of a heath bald on the ridge to your left. This "slick" (so-called because it looks smooth from a distance) is a mass of laurel and rhododendron so thick it's impassable for man or beast—large beasts,

anyway. Smaller creatures find shelter under its solid canopy, which crowds out all competition including trees.

In late spring and early summer such heath balds can become a mass of pink and white flowers.

● 12
THE CHANGING FOREST

Birches still dominate, but here and there are huge hemlocks many feet thick and perhaps a hundred feet high. Others in the community include maple, beech, and several varieties of oak; here and there you may spot the huge stump of an American chestnut, once the monarch of these woods. Logging and blight destroyed mature trees; saplings struggle from old roots, but they will not survive to maturity.

This is a forest in recovery from extensive logging. The land does heal, but its face is changed. In the competition of new growth, those pines and broad-leafed trees that grow quickly initially dominate the scene. In most cases they are slowly joined by the patient evergreens which, at higher elevations, eventually outnumber their deciduous cousins.

In their relative rush to a place in the sun, trees grow tall and thin, with leafy canopies thrust high atop pole-like, limbless trunks. In another setting many would take different shapes altogether. Life adapts as it must.

● 13

PIN OAK GAP

This is a small dip in the Balsam ridge. Until this point you've been headed generally north; now the road will bend sharply and head southwesterly toward Round Bottom. Changes will become apparent.

That's the way of the mountains. Aspect and altitude affect wind currents, rainfall, seasons, and the weather. You might run into rain or fog around one bend, sunshine around the next. You could drive from springtime on the ridge into summer in the lowlands, or up from late green summer down below into early golden fall. Or you may emerge from the cool shade of a north slope onto the sun-scorched side of a west-facing ridge.

As you leave the ridge from this point, the road heads down a deepening ravine where the Balsam (east) and Hyatt (west) ridges meet. Watch for visible changes in the forest community, even in the way the air feels.

So far the descent has been gradual; at Pin Oak Gap you're about 1,000 feet lower than back at Heintooga, where the graveled road began. Now the grade will be more apparent— not too demanding, but using second gear will make it easier on your brakes.

Left, from top: Galax; mountain laurel

Right: White-tailed buck in snow

● 14

HEADWATERS OF STRAIGHT FORK

Here's an especially refreshing spot to pause. Across the way a little cascade feeds the growing stream in a rush through rhododendron, mossy rocks, and deep woods. It's a good place to have the world to yourself for a little while.

These are the headwaters of Straight Fork, where cold, clear waters rise from numerous deep springs to start their long tumble down toward the lowland. It's an added treat that you'll follow their course all the way to its union with the Oconaluftee, back near Cherokee. Watch the growing river as you drive, the drips and trickles from small feeder springs and mini-waterfalls adding to the flow. Follow its gradual maturity from infant brook to noisy adolescent and robust maturity. The stream that nurtures so much life has a life of its own.

● 15
END OF ONE-WAY

This is the end of the one-way portion of the drive. The road's appearance doesn't change; traffic from the other direction is normally light, but use caution just in case. Passing places are provided along the one-lane section, and the road soon widens.

● 16
ROUND BOTTOM

At this point, perhaps you'll understand why the road has its odd nickname (Round Bottom). This is a broad, flat, "round" bottom. Take advantage of this pretty spot to stop and stroll and get better acquainted with the growing river.

From here down the road is straight and flat, and Straight Fork becomes that familiar mountain scene—huge mossy rocks in the streambed, the rush of whitewater, the lush abundance of riverside life.

● 17
PARK BOUNDARY

At the park boundary you're entering the Cherokee Reservation and an Indian community called Big Cove. The fish hatchery here stocks trout for the pleasure of the thousands who fish reservation waters, and provides useful income to the tribe.

Straight Fork joins Raven Fork just ahead. "Raven Fork," by the way, does not refer to the bird but to a great chief by that name (Kaluna, in Cherokee) who lived here during the time of the American Revolution.

Turn left at the road junction and it's nine miles back to Highway 441, right along the banks of Raven Fork, and scenic all the way. When you come to U.S. 441 you may turn right to head into the park—the Mountain Farm Museum and Oconaluftee Visitor Center—or turn left into Cherokee.

Left:
A fisherman tries his hand at some fishing in the Smokies

Right, from top: Rosebay rhododendron; a horseback rider enjoys the Smokies

Deep Creek & Lakeview Drive

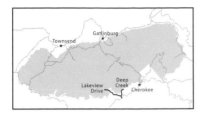

14 Miles
FROM CHEROKEE, NC TO
DEEP CREEK
CAMPGROUND

6 Miles
LAKEVIEW DRIVE

Two attractions lie near Bryson City, a quiet retreat from the busier resorts of Gatlinburg and Cherokee but no less rich in history. Once called "Bears Town," Bryson City was one of the earliest frontier settlements in the Smokies. Like the Deep Creek village nearby, it was a cluster of log homes in the shadow of the mountains in the early 1800s.

DEEP CREEK

Today this former community contains a park campground and picnic area among the dogwoods and beside the creek, just inside the park's southern boundary.

This well-developed campground is understandably popular, but sites are usually easier to find here than at the busier camps elsewhere in the park. Deep Creek is especially pretty in spring and fall. The campground is closed in winter, but the picnic area and hiking trails are open year-round.

The short trails from Deep Creek lead to delightful little Tom Branch and Juney Whank falls, or the great rush of Indian Creek Falls. All are easy walking (two miles round-trip at most) and can be reached by driving a quarter-mile past the campground entrance to the trailheads.

Left:
Indian Creek Falls

Right:
A park visitor enjoys Juney Whank Falls

LAKEVIEW DRIVE

From the middle of town in Bryson City, drive straight up the hill ahead instead of turning right toward Deep Creek. After 2.5 miles you'll re-enter the park, then wind among rising knobs that grow higher and higher on both sides, gorge-like.

The dead-end Lakeview Drive skirts the upper extremity of Fontana Lake, where the Tuckasegee River begins to widen and lose its identity in its growth, and the broad water below you glistens like a mirror among the deep green hills.

Left, from top:
View of Fontana
Lake; Noland Creek
bridge on Lakeview
Drive

Right, from top:
Backpackers hike
into the tunnel
beyond the end of
Lakeview Drive;
gateway to the
wilderness—the
Lakeshore Trail

● 1
FONTANA LAKE

This is the first of several scenic overlooks along this secluded drive. Look back toward the narrow lake filling the valley below. These are the uppermost waters of Fontana Lake, fed by the Tuckasegee River and impounded behind a dam about 25 miles downstream.

Fontana is one of the Tennessee Valley Authority's (TVAs) multipurpose dams, providing electric power, flood control, and recreation. It helps control the capricious and forceful runoff of waters from mountainside to flatlands by regulating its downstream flow, changing the lake's water level as its

gates are opened or closed. (Notice the different shore lines visible at the water's edge.) The lake, and the Little Tennessee River beyond it, marks the southwestern boundary of the park.

These steep hills and deep hollows often trap the rising mists in low clouds that settle above the river. In early morning especially, the sun can turn the "smoke" of the Smokies into a luminous veil, and a memorable view.

● 2
NOLAND CREEK BRIDGE

The bridge spans the deep cut of Noland Creek, whose cold, clear waters rise from a spring just below the summit of Clingmans

Dome, 5,000 feet farther up the mountainside. Noland Creek trail, which crosses here, could take you up the creek's course and along a high ridge all the way to the Dome, a 14-mile climb.

Downhill, the lake's edge is two miles distant. About halfway down is an especially pretty spot, where the rushing creek twists its way through a steep little gorge as it cascades toward Fontana.

● **3**

Road's End

The end of the road is the gateway to the wilderness. Stop and walk a bit. The trail past the gate leads through a tunnel, and ultimately across Forney Ridge to points west—interconnecting

with a network of foot trails that crisscross the roadless wild backcountry of the southwestern Smokies.

Remember that roads explore only a small percentage of the park's half-million acres. More than 800 miles of hiking trails make many other areas accessible. Even if you covered them all, by vehicle and on foot, you would have only sampled the wonder of this peerless preserve.

You may wonder how this dead-end road came to be. In the early 1940s, Fontana Lake flooded a state road north of the river; state, federal, and local authorities agreed that a new north shore road should be built to replace it. Construction began near Fontana Dam in 1949, and North Carolina completed a spur from Bryson City ten years later.

By that time, however, serious environmental and engineering concerns coalesced into public concern, and the upgrading of a south shore road had lessened the public need for the route.

Left:
Smoky Mountain
sunrise

Further construction proved not only difficult and expensive because of the tenuous geology, but controversial since it would disturb a roadless wild area in this part of the park. An alternative trans-mountain road across the park's west end was proposed in the 1960s, but quickly met opposition on similar grounds.

As a result, the plan has stalemated, with only this portion completed.

Flowering Tree & Fall Color Schedule

JANUARY—Witch hazel's bright yellow flowers linger from the previous year.

FEBRUARY—Red maple and spicebush bloom.

MARCH—Red bud and serviceberry trees bloom along Little River Road and in Cades Cove.

APRIL—Flowering dogwood, silverbell, and cucumber tree bloom.

MAY—Trees and shrubs in bloom include Fraser and umbrella magnolia, mountain laurel, tuliptree, yellowwood, sweet shrub, doghobble, and black locust. Serviceberry blooms along the Appalachian Trail.

JUNE—Rosebay rhododendron flowers at the lower elevations. Catawba rhododendron reaches its peak of bloom. White basswood blooms.

JULY—Rosebay rhododendron reaches its peak of bloom at the mid-elevations. Flame azalea flowers on Andrews and Gregory balds early in the month. Sourwood and Devil's walking stick bloom. Fruits mature on cucumber tree and Fraser magnolia.

AUGUST—Showy fruits mature on the following trees and shrubs: ironwood, witch hobble, staghorn sumac, and alternate-leaved dogwood. Witch hobble puts on the park's first fall leaf color.

SEPTEMBER—Trees showing early fall color include: flowering dogwood, black gum, sourwood, yellow birch, American beech, and pin cherry. Showy fruits mature on flowering dogwood, paw paw, black cherry, and American mountain-ash.

OCTOBER—Fall colors generally reach their peak between the 1st and 15th at the high elevations (above 4,500') and between the 16th and 31st at the mid and low elevations.

NOVEMBER—Oak leaves and other fall colors persist at the low elevations early in the month. Spiny sweetgum fruits are conspicuous on and around sweetgum trees.

DECEMBER—Red berries persist on American and mountain holly trees. Witch-hazel blooms.

PIGNUT HICKORY

FLOWERING DOGWOOD

NORTHERN RED OAK

SOURWOOD

SUGAR MAPLE

SILVERBELL

FRASER FIR

SWEETGUM

EASTERN HEMLOCK

Foothills Parkway

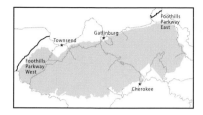

6 Miles
FOOTHILLS PARKWAY EAST

18 Miles
FOOTHILLS PARKWAY WEST

The Foothills Parkway is an unusual road since it's located outside the park, but is administratively part of it, and offers a panoramic perspective found nowhere else. The Parkway is in two segments: a six-mile spur connecting I-40 with State 32 near Cosby, and a 17.5-mile section from U.S. 321 north of Townsend, Tennessee to U.S. 129 at Chilhowee Reservoir. The two segments will be covered separately here.

This road, when completed, will be a 71-mile scenic drive through the Tennessee foothills. Construction began in 1960, with the State securing rights-of-way and transferring them to the Park Service. Further construction is now under way as funds become available.

Even segmented, the Foothills Parkway offers its own adventure; a scenic alternative approach to or departure from the Great Smokies. In this guide, both are followed east-to-west. (If you're driving in the opposite direction, simply follow the separate sections in reverse order.)

Left:
Foothills Parkway

Right:
Entrance to Foothills Parkway East

THE EAST END

From I-40 (21 miles east of its interchange with I-81) the Foothills Parkway exit (#443) is labeled as such. It's a short trip up and over Green Mountain with splendid views.

1

ENGLISH MOUNTAIN

Looking away from the park, the high ridge dominating the northern skyline is English Mountain (3,629 feet), about seven miles away. If it seems more imposing than its altitude suggests, that's because of the differences between these relatively modest elevations and the lowlands in between. These valleys are about 1,300 feet above sea level, so your view from here is like that from a 140-story skyscraper.

2

'HEART OF THE PARK' VIEW

Here your panoramic view is south. Get your bearings—in place and time—as you absorb the beauty. The high ridge in the distance is the heart of the park, the Appalachian Trail, the border between Tennessee and North Carolina. The first high knob above the gorge at left is Mt. Cammerer, with its lookout tower; farther to the right, in the misty distances, towers Mt. Guyot, second highest of the Smokies' peaks. Far to the right you may be able to pick out 6,593-foot Mt. Le Conte.

If you had some very special binoculars—the kind that look through time as well as space—you could watch a fascinating parade of human life across the lowlands beneath you. In the past, these fields and farmlands were a solid green

MT. CAMMERER
ELEVATION 4,928'

MT. GUYOT
ELEVATION 6,621'

carpet of virgin forest. But look carefully into the clearings—10,000 years ago there may have been a band of aboriginal hunters, spears poised, tracking a great herd of bison come to graze.

Change the focus to a later time: several Cherokee men afoot, their wives and children following, on a seasonal trip around the great mountains described as Sha-co-na-ge

("blue, like smoke") to fish and hunt the rich bounty of Ga-da-lu-tsi (now Cataloochee).

And more recently still: several horse-drawn wagons appear headed west. They're loaded with household goods and a few family treasures. Driven by hopeful Euro-American settlers, the wagons have come from the Carolinas, around the "Great Iron Mountains," creaking toward an unknown frontier settlement called "Sugarlands."

Footpaths instead of roads then crossed the valley, which was filled with forests instead of farms. Much changes, and the changes continue to the present. But the mountains endure.

Whether this is your first view of the Great Smokies on arrival, or your last on leaving, let the scene sink in.

The West End

This 18-mile drive follows the crest of Chilhowee (pronounced "chil-HOW-ee") Mountain, an unusually long and uniform wrinkle in the plain beyond the Great Smokies. Its western terminus is the shore of Chilhowee Reservoir. There it connects with U.S. 129 about 22 miles south of Maryville, Tennessee.

Chilhowee is an unusual mountain: one continuous narrow ridge almost 30 miles long and 2,700 feet high, from the Little Tennessee River on the southwest to near Sevierville on the northeast. It's notched in the middle, a steep, short gorge cut by the Little River on its way to the Tennessee at Knoxville.

The Parkway's west segment begins at U.S. 321, nine miles from the park entrance at Townsend, following the lower end of the mountain to Chilhowee Reservoir. From its vantage point, the road offers excellent views of the Smokies to the south and the sudden flatlands of the Tennessee valley northward.

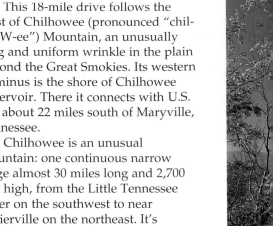

**Miller Cove,
Elevation 960'**

*Left:
Millers Cove sunrise*

*Right, from top:
Look Rock Tower;
Pitch pine*

● **3**

Miller Cove

You'll find no better views of the great bulk of the Smokies than that from several Foothills overlooks. In the southeastern distance, 22 miles away, you might be able to pick out Clingmans Dome, the park's highest peak.

The lowlands below you are another of those relatively flat geologic oddities called a cove. Miller Cove—about eight miles long and scarcely a mile wide—is a fertile lowland bounded by the abrupt rise of Chilhowee Mountain on one side and the knobby foothills of the Smokies on the other.

Just east of here the ancient Little River, which began in springs high on Clingmans Dome, makes a sheer and dramatic slice through the middle of Chilhowee Mountain, providing easy passage for U.S. 321 between Maryville, Tennessee and the park entrance at Townsend.

The Foothills Parkway will ultimately continue easterly atop the ridges to your left to join its eastern segment, 33 miles away.

● 4

BLACK SULPHUR KNOBS

This overlook offers an outstanding view across the flatlands toward Maryville and the Tennessee Valley. The uniform little knobs below you mark the last surge of foothills before the land levels.

Those to the left are called the Woodpeckers, and the mound-like hillocks nearest are the Black Sulphur Knobs. Your view is northwest: Maryville is six miles distant, and Knoxville a little to the right and 20 miles away.

● 5

WARRIOR'S PATH

The broad flatlands between Maryville and Knoxville were once—until the removal of the Cherokee on the "Trail of Tears" in 1838—the route of the Great Warriors' Path (or "War Path"). This was the main "highway," with many interconnecting branches, between scattered Cherokee settlements from as far south as Georgia and Alabama north to the Ohio River.

Despite its name, the Warriors' Path was mostly a peaceful route of commerce and communication—although it was also the route used to wage war with other tribes. It crossed the Little Tennessee not far from today's terminus of the Foothills Parkway and ran northeasterly toward what's now Bristol. There it turned northwesterly through the Cumberland Gap into Kentucky. Branches led into Tuckaleechee and other areas, including a route along the Pigeon River at the east end of the Smokies into North Carolina.

6

LOOK ROCK

A high point of the parkway, literally and figuratively, is this observation ledge called Look Rock. Here's a marvelous sweep of the Great Smokies—Gregory Bald to your right, Thunderhead to the left. Cades Cove Mountain and the Cerulean Knob in the left foreground.

For an even better view—a 360-degree panorama—take the short (half-mile) trail across the road. It leads to a sturdy lookout tower atop the mountain.

7

HAPPY VALLEY VIEWPOINT

As you pause here to enjoy the sweeping view, Gregory Bald dominates the peaks at the park's western edge. In the lowland to the left of Gregory, hidden by the near ridges, lies Cades Cove. Farther left, your view is directly up the high ridge of mainline Smokies toward the heart of the park.

The lowland immediately below you is called Happy Valley, drained by Abrams Creek—the same one that flows through Cades Cove. Weeping willows and mimosa dot its banks, both Asian immigrants that have found a comfortable home in Happy Valley.

Such non-native species of plants and animals (called "exotics,") create a constant and expensive problem for the country's national parks. Of great concern here in the Smokies is the wild hog, a European pig that escaped from a North Carolina game preserve and became established in the park in the late 1940s.

Left:
Foothills Parkway

Right:
Sunrise viewed from Foothills Parkway West

GREGORY BALD, ELEVATION 4,948'

The hog is an omnivorous animal with no natural enemies in the park. Its voracious rooting destroys or endangers plants, insects, small animals—many already rare, some found only here. An unknown number—perhaps 500 or more—of these invaders now forage over most of the park's acreage.

Their long-term effect on soil erosion, water pollution, competition with indigenous wildlife, and other impacts are still being studied. So are ways to stop the hog's relentless spread and to curtail its destruction.

It's a problem that's worthy of your attention. This is your park, after all, and things that threaten this national treasure—wild hogs, ground-level ozone pollution, woolly adelgids and others—deserve your awareness and concern.

● 8
GREAT SMOKIES' FAULT

As you consider the sweeping views visible along your route, stop a moment to think about what you don't see. The hidden earth beneath your feet has created the spectacle, and Chilhowee is evidence of those vital dynamics.

Chilhowee is a long ridge that traces exactly the Great Smokies Fault—that meeting-of-the-plates along which opposing slabs move to force great upheaval and mountain-building. That geologic turbulence happened here many millions of years ago and was infinitesimally slow, so "riding the fault" is not as ominous as it sounds. Minor

GREGORY BALD

Named for Russell Gregory (1795-1864) and his wife, Susan, believed to be the third white family to settle in the Cades Cove area. The couple settled on Gregory Bald in the 1820s and raised livestock. They later moved down to Cades Cove. Russell Gregory lost his life during the Civil War at the hands of Confederate raiders operating out of North Carolina.

tremors do occasionally occur in this region, however.

Imagine two bricks, one atop the other. Tilt the bottom bricks and the one on top slides a bit. That's a simplified picture of plate movements beneath the earth's visible surface—except that these "bricks" are gigantic plates bound in completely by other

Left:
Red dawn from
Foothills Parkway

rock masses and subjected to enormous pressure on all sides. When one brick moves, something obviously has to give, so we have earthquakes and mountains.

You won't find fossils in most rocks of the Great Smokies. That's because the bulk of the mountains was already formed before hard-bodied plants and animals developed. Here along the fault line, however soft limestone has pushed its way to the surface, and primitive fossils have been found.

These aren't anything so dramatic as dinosaur bones; you probably wouldn't recognize one if you saw it, without special skills and a large magnifying glass. The fossils here are the remains of primitive plants and animals that had developed hard parts— ancestors of clams and snails, for instance— during the Early Cambrian geologic period more than 450 million years ago.

Smoky Mountain Elevations

CLINGMANS DOME	6,643 FEET
MOUNT GUYOT	6,621 FEET
MOUNT LE CONTE (HIGH TOP)	6,593 FEET
MOUNT BUCKLEY	6,580 FEET
MOUNT LOVE	6,420 FEET
MOUNT CHAPMAN	6,417 FEET
OLD BLACK	6,370 FEET
LUFTEE KNOB	6,234 FEET
MOUNT KEPHART	6,217 FEET
MOUNT COLLINS	6,188 FEET
ANDREWS BALD	5,920 FEET
CHARLIES BUNION	5,565 FEET
NEWFOUND GAP	5,046 FEET
ALUM CAVE BLUFFS	4,970 FEET
SPENCE FIELD	4,920 FEET
CHIMNEY TOPS	4,800 FEET
RAMSEY CASCADES	4,300 FEET
CATALOOCHEE VALLEY	2,680 FEET
LAUREL FALLS	2,600 FEET
OCONALUFTEE VISITOR CENTER	2,040 FEET
CADES COVE VISITOR CENTER	1,716 FEET
SUGARLANDS VISITOR CENTER	1,462 FEET

Index

Credits

PHOTOGRAPHY

Kent Cave: iv (flower), 35 (horse), 47

Kendall Chiles: 26, 58 (field), 120 (lily), 146

Harry Ellis: 101 (geranium)

Jessie M. Harris: 101 (bloodroot), 128 (galax)

John Heidecker: iv (road), 24 (columbine), 83 (iris)

Adam Jones: front cover (road), back cover (butterfly), inside cover
(lane), 20 (road), 61 (lane), 101 (phalencia), 135 (road), 138, 144

Byron Jorjorian: 14 (hikers), 73 (woodpecker), 89 (salamander)

Mary Ann Kressig: 10, 14 (road), 24 (road, view), 34 (apple house),
35 (kitchen, house), 39 (firs), 50 (falls), 58 (cabin), 60 (view), 61
(tombstone), 62, 72, 80, 83 (tub mill), 85 (river), 86 (falls), 87, 91
(road), 92 (corncrib, barn), 93, 97, 102, 108 (barn, church), 111
(house), 114 (footbridge), 122 (campground), 124, 126 (trail),
131 (horseback riders), 133

Jay Kranyik: 126 (plant)

Bill Lea: front cover (bear), inside cover (Rich Mountain Road, road
through Cataloochee), 13 (picnic area), 14 (flowers), 16, 17
(stream), 18-19, 20 (landslide), 21, 22 (view, memorial), 25, 27
(sunset), 30 (stream), 31 (picnic area), 32, 33 (mill chute,
building), 36, 38 (trail), 39 (firs), 40 (tower), 41 (forest), 42-45, 46
(water), 48 (school, fisherman), 49, 51 (quiet walkway), 52-57,
59, 60 (church, butterfly), 61 (church), 63 (building), 64, 65
(cabin), 66-67, 68 (deer, road), 70-71, 73 (deer), 74 (bear), 75-76,
78 (town), 81-82, 89 (photographer, cabin), 94, 95 (river), 96,
98-100, 101 (squirrel corn, hepatica, iris), 103 (road), 104-05, 107
(creek, bridge), 113 (house), 116-17, 118, 120 (view), 121, 123,
127 (view), 128 (flowers), 129, 132, 134, 135 (hikers), 136, 139,
140, 141 (view), 142, 143 (tower), 145

Ken McFarland: 127 (flowers)

Don McGowan: back cover (road), 7

Ed Ponikwia: 101 (phlox, Bishop's cap, bluets)

Shelly Powell: front cover (post)

Nye Simmons: 15 (trees), 65 (cabin), 84 (falls), 86 (boys), 91 (cabin),
95 (flowers)

Ken Voorhis: 22 (plant), 24 (leaves), 27 (flowers), 30 (leaves), 31
(flower), 34 (flowers), 40 (flowers), 65 (flowers), 68 (flowers), 74
(road), 85 (newt), 103 (leaves), 122 (branch), 131 (flowers), 137,
141 (branch), 143 (branch)

Charles Webb: 13 (view), 130

All historic photographs courtesy of the National Park Service.

SUPPLEMENTAL TEXT SOURCES

Excerpts of this book obtained from *Place Names of the Smokies*
with permission by Allen R. Coggins.

Other Guides to the Smokies

T he following books, guides, and videos will help you explore the rich natural and cultural history of Great Smoky Mountains National Park and will enrich your visit to the Smokies immeasurably. These titles may be purchased at sales areas in the visitor centers, online at www.SmokiesStore.org, or by phoning (865) 436-7318.

GREAT SMOKY MOUNTAINS NATIONAL PARK MOVIE
This is the "official park movie" shown at Sugarlands Visitor Center. 20 minutes. VHS Item #200091; DVD Item #200150

PARK MAP/GUIDES
These park folders feature full-color maps which highlight roads and trails of interest. The reverse sides offer color photos, charts, detail maps, safety information, and more.

- Auto Touring
- Trees & Forests
- Backpack Loops
- Waterfalls
- Day Hikes
- Wildflowers
- Geology
- Wildlife Viewing
- Historic Areas
- Birds & Birding

HIKING TRAILS OF THE SMOKIES
A comprehensive guide to the official trails in Great Smoky Mountains National Park. Covers all 150 maintained trails with detailed narratives including highlights of each trail, local history and lore, and special cautions to be wary of when hiking. Includes a full color, all-park trip planning map plus 165 trail profile charts indicating the length and elevation changes of each trail. Handy, pocket size (6" x 4 1/2"). Printed on special lightweight paper for easy packing. Softcover, 584 pages, weighs 11 oz. Item #400161